Learning and Teaching Business

Peter Lorange

Learning and Teaching Business

Lessons and Insights from a Lifetime of Work

Peter Lorange
IMD
Lausanne, Switzerland

ISBN 978-3-031-14563-6   ISBN 978-3-031-14564-3   (eBook)
https://doi.org/10.1007/978-3-031-14564-3

© The Editor(s) (if applicable) and The Author(s), under exclusive licence to Springer Nature Switzerland AG 2022
This work is subject to copyright. All rights are solely and exclusively licensed by the Publisher, whether the whole or part of the material is concerned, specifically the rights of translation, reprinting, reuse of illustrations, recitation, broadcasting, reproduction on microfilms or in any other physical way, and transmission or information storage and retrieval, electronic adaptation, computer software, or by similar or dissimilar methodology now known or hereafter developed.
The use of general descriptive names, registered names, trademarks, service marks, etc. in this publication does not imply, even in the absence of a specific statement, that such names are exempt from the relevant protective laws and regulations and therefore free for general use.
The publisher, the authors, and the editors are safe to assume that the advice and information in this book are believed to be true and accurate at the date of publication. Neither the publisher nor the authors or the editors give a warranty, expressed or implied, with respect to the material contained herein or for any errors or omissions that may have been made. The publisher remains neutral with regard to jurisdictional claims in published maps and institutional affiliations.

This Springer imprint is published by the registered company Springer Nature Switzerland AG.
The registered company address is: Gewerbestrasse 11, 6330 Cham, Switzerland

Preface

Many of you may legitimately ask me "why this book? Isn't it simply another autobiography? Or, a restatement of management principles, many of which are already well known? If so, why should I have an interest in reading it?" I would like to tell you that you are *not* holding an autobiography or a treatise of management principles in your hand. Rather, this is a book about how to come up with better performance for business organizations, and, corresponding with this, improved curricula for leading academic institutions, drawing on a set of reflections from my long experience in academia and business. I believe that experience-based reflections tend to be both more interesting *and* more useful than mere chronological, biographical ones, or conceptual reviews of management dimensions without links to practice.

While many authors have discussed strategic vision, both as it relates to business and to academia, the authors who are perhaps coming closest to my own views are Dewar, Keller, and Malhotra (2022) with their six elements of an effective CEO vision. I am however relatively more focused on the importance of what might be seen as one's own personal core values than these authors.

The impetus for this book came from several sources. Having been centrally involved in executive education at a number of leading academic institutions for several decades, I have come to realize that the very design of an institution's curriculum is of central importance for ensuring

v

vi   Preface

more effective learning. My long-time friend, Bjørg Kibsgaard-Petersen, has urged me to put down on paper a set of thoughts such as these for a long time. My friend and former colleague, Dag Sandborg, argued convincingly that a set of generalizations based on my experiences, such as those I will share with you in this book, would probably be of broader interest. I have also put together a considerable art collection and have been thinking about how to draw on my experience in doing this. Finally, having recently transferred the ownership of my online education business, Lorange Network, to IMD, and most of what I own to my two children, I felt that it might be useful for all these stakeholders to have this set of guidelines to refer to.

Now to the methodology that has guided me. Having been inspired by Proust as well as Lehrer, I recognize that when revisiting events years after they actually took place, they can tend to appear "rosier" than they may actually have been. Or as Lehrer has said:

"... there simply is no way to describe the past without lying. Our memories are not *like* fiction. They *are* fiction" (Lehrer, 2007). There is clearly a "warning" to me here: can I be relatively objective? There is probably very little, if any evidence that one's life and career stages can be planned out. Rather, much of what many of us have experienced in our careers could be seen as quite random. However, there may also be an element of rationality when it comes to "revisiting" the various chapters in one's career. While one may often feel as if things simply (and randomly) happen, there might also be an element of more deliberately *positioning* oneself for certain events, i.e., being ready (being there) when an opportunity arises. Hence, there might be some sort of pattern in the evolution of one's career after all. Rorty addresses this dilemma as follows: "To say that we should drop the idea of truth as out there waiting to be discovered is not to say that we have discovered that, out there, there is no truth" (Rorty, 1989).

So, is there a way to cope with these dilemmas? Was Jane Austen right? "Seldom, very seldom, does complete truth belong to any human disclosure; seldom can it happen that something is not a little disguised or a little mistaken" (Austen, 1999). Still, my sense is that it might be worthwhile trying to make some "semi-objective" sense out of the past, finding solace in T.S. Elliot ("only those who will risk going too far can possibly find out how far one can go" (1931)), and in Marianne Moore ("psychology, which explains everything, explains nothing" (1967)).

This book has been written with the above considerations in mind. It is divided into four parts. In Part one, I chronicle what seem to me to be major steps or markers in my life experiences as well as the key influences on the development of my thinking. These four chapters consist largely of autobiographical highlights, including covering some of my key research contributions. I attempt to draw conclusions based on these experiences for managing academic institutions as well as businesses in better ways, and for effective curriculum design for business schools of the future. In Part two, I provide reflections on various aspects of my working life in business. These three chapters draw out what have been the most significant developments during the various phases of my career, particularly when it comes to the running of my various business activities. Then, in Parts three and four, I provide examples of some of the key principles and skills that have guided me and which I have come to regard as essential. Finally, in Part four I articulate what seem to be a few types of skills that might be particularly important for strengthening performance in business organizations. The book concludes with my final thoughts on how these ideas translate into a better business school curriculum.

As I have said, this book is about my vision for improving business, as well as for making higher education better, of greater relevance, and more cost-effective. As has been pointed out, "having a vision is like looking at the present from the future's standpoint" (Konovalov, 2021, p. xviii), i.e., "translating a positive image of the future into reality" (Goldsmith, quoted by Konovalov, 2021, p.23). In the following pages I have attempted, in a modest way, to do exactly this. This vision emerged only gradually. It was shaped over many years by the journey I have gone through. More will be discovered about effective curriculum design in the future. As Konovalov observes (p. 27), "vision doesn't come overnight but as a result of years of focused thinking looking for a solution to a serious challenge." This trajectory for vision-setting is indeed what I have been going through! The "serious challenge" for me has been to ultimately come up with a vision for business as well as for higher quality

viii   Preface

education which might also be effective relative to the costs of achieving this.

In order to produce a version of a vision that is relatively concrete, this book examines the key experiences that have impacted on the shaping of the vision – not only my experiences in academia, but also various impacts from my upbringing as well as from my career in business. My experiences in academic research and publishing have perhaps been particularly important in this vision-shaping process. I discuss this particularly in Part one, i.e., how my various research endeavors have impacted on the choice of the various dimensions that constitute my vision. Readers might find it surprising that I have raked through an entire set of issues about "my life," which might traditionally be seen as some sort of autobiography. My sense, however, is that this "journey" has been absolutely central when it comes to the shaping of my vision. That is really the reason for including Part one in this book!

I would like to share three additional reflections on this evolutionary journey, particularly as they relate to what is presented in Part one. My sense of what quality-based higher education should be evolved gradually from relying primarily, and perhaps to too great a degree, on memorizing rather than trying to learn: from last-minute "cramming" rather than fundamental learning. This seems to largely have been the case in my own school years. Then, from frankly often finding lecturers to be uninspiring and thus relying largely on self-study, from gradually appreciating the benefits of dialogue in auditorium settings, from being frustrated with at times relatively incompetent lecturers to increasingly appreciating the power of cutting-edge professors regarding the learning process, and so on. My sense of what effective learning could thus gradually come to include a realization that the context for learning matters!

While many of the key influences on my development, involving both family members and non-family colleagues and friends (see Chap. 4), do not provide direct links to the shaping of my vision, they are still critical to that vision, particularly in conditioning me to be more open-minded, searching, and always ready to continue to learn. In some cases, some of these key inspirational sources directly added to the shaping of my vision, in particular my father's emphasis on the fundamental importance of education, as well as my grandfather's emphasis on creativity and entrepreneurship.

The central part of the book represents a delineation of a set of critical success factors, which are key for achieving business success, in my opinion. Each of these factors, discussed in Parts two and three and four, derive from my career experience, stemming from leadership of my own businesses, consulting, and board activities. The book also provides insights regarding how good business practices might be taught in modern business schools. Curriculum design might be improved through adopting the guidelines reproduced in this book. It is essential to promote the importance of a strong corporate culture, as reflected by the set of critical success factors. Good curriculum design should draw on solid business practices.

Allow me a few final reflections that have emerged during the writing of this book.

Honest communication seems key! And while it can be hard, and even brutal, to be perfectly honest, I have tried to do this. My sense is that the more information one shares with others, the better, as is, perhaps above all, highlighted by the relatively broad networks of people that have been involved in Lorange Institute as well as Lorange Network. The bulk of these network members might indeed be considered as "ambassadors" when it comes to promulgating the vision that is being proposed.

So, in conclusion, "why did you write this book?" is a pertinent question. The short answer would be to try to come up with a clearer vision for what high-quality advanced education might entail. This was my primary motivation for writing this book. So the effort put into the writing of it should certainly not be seen as "an ego trip." While a somewhat systematic autobiographical account might perhaps become of interest to future generations of family and to my friends, this has not been the key driver behind what is to follow. In the end, does my concern for future generations play a central role when it comes to the writing of this book? Yes, it is this group of stakeholders that would benefit from a better future learning environment, i.e., from my vision coming to fruition.

Küssnacht am Rigi, Switzerland   Peter Lorange
July 2022

Acknowledgments

There are many individuals who have inspired me and have thereby contributed to this book, and they all deserve my thanks. Above all, these include the many people I have had encounters with, as reported in this book. I have tried to be fair and balanced here. To those who feel that I have perhaps misrepresented them, I apologize, as this was unintentional on my part. And then there are those who have offered specific suggestions and comments. These include my two sisters, Helene and Anne, my daughter Anne Sophie and her husband Frode, my son Per Frithjof and his wife Kristin, my cousin Kirsten Frederiksen and her husband Frithjof, IMD's President, Dr. Jean-Francois Manzoni, my former colleague at IMD for many years, Dr. Jim Ellert, and of course, my close friend Bjørg Kibsgaard-Petersen. Thanks a lot, to all of you! Special thanks too to Karin Mugnaini, President of Lorange Network. There are clearly others who also should have been singled out for thanks. Please allow me to thank them in general. Finally, Leda Nishino did a large part of the typing, and my personal assistant, Lizzie Schwegler-Ellis, also did a lot of typing, as well as significant editing. She deserves special thanks. Her help in putting this all together has been invaluable. And, as always, Paula Parish did a superb editing job.

Contents

Part I How Was My Vision Shaped? 1

1 Upbringing and Education 3
Early Childhood in Slemmestad 3
Youth in Asker 4
Norwegian School of Economics and Business
Administration (1962–1964) 5
Education—General Reflections 6
Studies in the United States (1967–1971) 7
Yale (1967–1968) 7
Harvard Business School (HBS) (1968–1972) 8
Key Learnings 8

**2 Experiences from Academia and Academic
Administration** 11
Academic Posts 11
IMEDE (1971–1973) 11
MIT's Sloan School of Management (1973–1980) 12
Wharton (1980–1989) 13
Stockholm School of Economics (SSE) (1983–1984) 13

xiii

xiv   Contents

Roles in Academic Administration	14
MIT's Sloan School of Management	14
Wharton (1985–1990)	14
Norwegian School of Business (BI) (1989–1993)	14
IMD (1993–2008)	15
The Transition to IMD	15
Business Development	17
Faculty Management	18
Succession	19
Family Considerations	21
Commandore, the Royal Norwegian Order of Merited Services (2010)	22
Key Learnings	22

3 The Role of Research — 25

Fields of Research	25
Shipping	26
Family Business	27
Strategic Planning	27
Top Line and Bottom Line	28
Educational	29
Key Learnings	31

4 Influences from Family and Friends — 33

Influences from Family Members	33
Influences from Friends and Colleagues	39
Key Learnings	43

Part II   The Influence of Business — 45

5 Lorange Institute and Lorange Network — 47

Lorange Institute (2012–2017)	47
Lorange Network (2017–2021)	50
Key Learnings	52

Contents   xv

6 Family Business Strategies   55
S. Ugelstad Rederi (SUR)   55
S. Ugelstad Invest (SUI) (2009–2021)   57
Other Family Business Activities   61
   Olsen and Ugelstad, Oslo (Shipowners)   61
   A/S Sydfjell, as well as Real Estate Properties in
   Ulvøysund and Salmeli   61
   Store Stabekk (Hövik, Norway)   62
Key Learnings   62

7 Board Membership and Consulting Assignments   65
Boards   65
   Kvaerner (Oslo/London)   66
   Knud I. Larsen (Copenhagen): Diversified Shipping
   Company   67
   Royal Caribbean Cruise Lines (RCCL) (Miami)   67
   Seaspan (Vancouver/Hong Kong)   67
   ISS (Copenhagen)   68
   Citicorp Norway/International (Oslo, London)   68
   Copenhagen Business School   69
   Co Co Co (Copenhagen)   69
   IKO Strategi (Oslo)   70
   Globalpraxis (Barcelona)   70
   Keystone (Oslo)   71
Consulting   71
   Ericsson Radio (Stockholm)   72
   San Miguel (Manila)   73
   Elkem (Oslo)   73
   Borregaard (Sarpsborg)   75
   Norsk Hydro (Oslo)   75
   Michelin (Clermont-Ferrand, France)   76
   Tine (and previously Øglaend, Sandnes) (Oslo)   76
   Pechiney (Paris)   77
Key Learnings   77

xvi   Contents

Part III   Guiding Principles   81

8   Quality of Education, Career, Business, and Art   85
Educational Choices   85
Jobs   87
Business   91
Art   93
Residences   94
Why Live in Switzerland?   95
Quality and Business School Curricula   97
Key Learnings   98

9   Diversity Is Key!   99
Academia   100
Research   102
Curriculum Design   103
The Arts   104
Business   105
Sports   107
Key Learnings   109

10   The Importance of Managing Risk and Uncertainty   111
Due Diligence   112
How Much Should We Invest?   116
How Early Should One Invest?   117
Taking Profits   117
Key Learnings   117

11   Discipline and Integrity in Decision-Making   119
Examples of Focused Decision-Making   120
Targeting   121
Examples of Challenges to Honesty and Integrity   123
Value Profile   125
Key Learnings   126

Contents xvii

Part IV   Business Skills 129

12   Networking: An Emerging and Ongoing Dictum 131
"Give More than You Take" 131
Examples of Network Strategies 134
Norwegian School of Business (BI) 134
Lorange Institute (LI) 135
Lorange Network 135
IMD 135
Marsoft 136
Keystone 136
Globalpraxis 136
Broader Implications 137
Key Learnings 137

13   The Importance of Gaining and Maintaining Speed 139
Operational Clarity 140
Strategic Clarity 141
Avoid "Micro-Management" 142
Immediate Follow-Up 143
Key Learnings 144

14   Proactivity, Positivity, and Innovation 147
Examples of Open-Minded, Positive Thinking in Practice 148
Innovation 149
Key Learnings 152

15   Cycle Management: Entries and Exits 153
Decision-Making in Cycle Management 154
Examples of Cycle Management 155
Shipping 156
Real Estate 157
Stocks 157
The Timing of IPOs 158
Key Learnings 158

xviii   Contents

Part V   Conclusions   161

16   Learning in the Future: Individuals, Business, and
Academic Institutions   163
Business Schools of the Future: Effective Curricula   167
Modern Organizations and Educational Institutions:
Principles and Skills   169
Final Words   170

Books Authored   173

References   175

Part I

How Was My Vision Shaped?

This first section of the book discusses each of the four major forces that have shaped my vision when it comes to what constitutes good business practice, as well as effective curriculum design at institutions of business education. My upbringing and education naturally represent an important source of inspiration. My career, both academic as well as professional, is equally important. And research has certainly also contributed a lot to the shaping of my vision. Finally, particular influencers, some of whom are family members and others who are not, have been critically important.

Thus, there is a particular blend of factors that seem to have had a bearing on the development of my own vision, in contrast to what some leading academicians and philosophers might suggest. For instance, the ancient Chinese philosopher, Lao Tzu, believes that to focus on less is of key importance: "The journey of a thousand miles begins with a single step".

1

Upbringing and Education

Early Childhood in Slemmestad

I grew up in Slemmestad, a small industrial town around 50 km outside of Oslo, Norway. The prevailing culture in Slemmestad during the 1940s and 1950s was "classical" and traditional, quite similar to what Lahlum (2019) describes when it comes to another industrial society, Hurum in Norway, where the Norwegian Labor politician Reiulf Steen grew up. Both communities were relatively isolated, being some distance from Oslo, and there were clear norms, often built around socialist, even communist ideological principles. Thus, there was a high degree of solidarity between workers and, one might say, a fairly tight-knit culture. In contrast, local bureaucrats and their families sat largely outside the above-mentioned community, representing a looser culture. Needless to say, there was a lot of tension between these two subcultures, and even latent conflicts (Lahlum). For an individual to feel comfortable, they would have to adhere to the norms ("be normal, not snobbish").

Many of us ski jumped in the garden at Nesset where we lived. This was great fun for all of us children, and we were typically reluctant to come indoors and eat our (early) dinner when called by our mothers.

© The Author(s), under exclusive license to Springer Nature Switzerland AG 2022
P. Lorange, *Learning and Teaching Business*,
https://doi.org/10.1007/978-3-031-14564-3_1

And there were band (gentle gangs) "wars" between the children who lived around my family home, Nesset, most of whom were relatively well off, and the children from the mostly working class families, such as those from Heimann, an area of the town. These skirmishes were normally quite harmless: we "fought" with sticks only. But there were times when we exchanged our sticks for homemade bows and arrows, as well as slings. The ammunition here was "blubbers," small metal pieces collected from the cement grinding mills. It was quite dangerous actually.

My parents were Elisabeth (née Ugelstad) and Per. And I had two sisters, Helene, born in 1946, and Anne, born in 1951. I will describe my family in more detail in Chap. 4 and explain what they both meant and mean to me.

Youth in Asker

At around the age of 14, my family and I moved to our new home in nearby Asker. I found it difficult to move from Slemmestad to Asker and it was particularly difficult to make new friends. The upside, looking back, is that I was suddenly faced with more "diversity" and many open-minded, "smart" new people. I may not have fully valued this aspect until much later. In junior high, as well as in high school, at Asker Realskole and Gymnas, I remember having to memorize my lessons, as opposed to fundamental learning, with last-minute cramming during the breaks between classes, including writing notes and translations in textbooks, especially when it came to French and Old Norwegian. My favorite subject was the Norwegian—language and literature. This passion for writing and reading has stayed with me ever since.

My parents often asked me how things were going at school. They were always interested in my grade sheets. I typically received a lot of praise and positive feedback from them, as well as small amounts of money from my grandfather for good grades and notable achievements. I recall receiving private tutoring in English and in mathematics. My parents paid for all of this.

I often felt a sense of anxiety during my upbringing, which at times was relatively high. For instance, when I was a teenager, it seemed particularly important for me to be included in the activities of groups of youngsters of my own age. And I still remember those setbacks. For instance, in Slemmestad, when I was around 13 years old, I was not invited to a neighbor's party. I was perhaps deemed to be somewhat "immature." It hurt! When our family moved to Asker, we typically spent weekends at our family's cottage in Ådalen, around 90 minutes away. This deprived me of mingling with other teenagers and I felt frustrated by this. In retrospect, I have come to realize that being able to cope with such frustrations is key to many aspects of being successful.

After completing high school in 1961, I took a one-year crash course in basic business, economics, and commercial law at Oslo Commercial High School, and was then admitted to the Norwegian School of Economics and Business Administration (NHH) in Bergen. I was only 20 years old, i.e., much younger than most of the others in my class, partly because I was exempted from the at that time compulsory military service in Norway due to a medical mishap I had suffered many years earlier, when my spleen had to be removed, age seven.

Norwegian School of Economics and Business Administration (1962–1964)

I was clearly not mature enough when I started at NHH at the age of 20. I think that I was also too socially immature to be able to benefit fully from this opportunity. Most of my fellow students were significantly older than me, and I guess I felt this age difference. However, I did well, once more largely by memorizing facts rather than by a "deeper" form of analytical thinking. I did not learn much and lacked in-depth under-standing. This may, however, have prepared the ground for me in later years, when I fully embraced the concept of learning by doing, as opposed to just talking about it!

I chose to study Economic Geography at NHH as one of two elective study areas (1962–1964). At that time, NHH did not offer Strategy as a field of study. Cultural (economic) geography was the closest they had, with a particular focus on key issues relating to industry locations and other patterns of economic activities. While I must admit that this choice of study was perhaps more intuitive than deliberate, perhaps even impulsive, it still gave me a great introduction to the field of Strategy, an area that I have pursued ever since, and an interest that I have kept up to this day.

A contributing factor in my choice of area of study was the professor in charge of Economic Geography at NHH, Professor Dr. Axel Sømme, who was an exceptionally inspiring person, particularly because of his readiness to dialogue with young students such as me (see Chap. 4). This course and this professor also introduced me to the insight that active interaction between teachers and students is key, something that I have attempted to put into practice ever since.

It should be noted that Dr. Sømme also offered me a position as his research assistant for a year from 1966 to 1967, involving me in a project to evaluate the impact on nature of large hydroelectric power developments. This focus on nature conservation has remained an area of concern for me ever since then and is perhaps particularly relevant today when it comes to the emission of gases into our atmosphere, as well as the pollution of our oceans from plastics, for instance (Anker, 2020).

Education—General Reflections

I always felt that I could count on the full backing of my parents when it came to my studies. They paid for my education at NHH, i.e., board and tuition, although there was not much of a welfare state in Norway at that time and gave me a television set as well as a car (a Mini). They also gave me carte blanche to study for my doctorate at Yale (where I took a Master's in Operations Analysis, 1968) and subsequently at Harvard (for my Doctor of Business Administration, obtained in 1972). The issue of funding was never discussed. In the end, I was able to cover the costs of these studies through stipends (from the Ford Foundation, largely). But clearly, the relatively affluent and supportive culture of my family allowed me to take the risk of pursuing higher education in the United States.

In contrast, most students would at that time have had to cover the financial burden of their graduate studies themselves, perhaps through loans from a Norwegian agency set up for this (Statens Låssekasse), as well as partly by other means. Most were faced with more constraining cultural settings, however. I, therefore, feel both fortunate and grateful to my parents for their steadfast support of my studies.

As I noted at the start of this chapter, economic strength fosters a relatively *looser* culture and, consequently, one has a greater capacity to take risks, i.e., to pursue innovative paths which might entail taking more risks. The fact that I entered relatively risky programs of study at Yale and Harvard reflects this, with the economic uncertainties that this entailed. Further, for me to later take on relatively risky job assignments as President of the Norwegian School of Business (BI) and then IMD can be better understood in the context of what might be seen as my economic independence, i.e., knowing that I would always have something to fall back on if things did not work out. I simply did not need these jobs to live but, rather, I was in a position to do what I felt was right without worrying about the potentially adverse effects of losing my job or the dysfunctional economic efforts of having to quit. This may also have been a factor when I took on the risky attempt to test out what might turn out to be "the business school of the future," i.e., Lorange Institute and Lorange Network (see Chap. 5). My economic independence made it easier for me to take on these substantial financial commitments. In the end, it turned out that I was more than largely compensated for these efforts. In summary, in my professional activities and later my business activities I have probably been able to take several courses of action that I most likely would not have pursued had I not been relatively independently well off.

Studies in the United States (1967–1971)

Yale (1967–1968)

I first entered the doctoral program at Yale with the intention of taking my doctorate in operations analysis. But this program turned out to be extremely specialized, particularly in mathematics, and even though the kind of mathematics that was taught there could be described as applied,

8 P. Lorange

it became clear to me that the material was difficult for me to meaningfully comprehend and not all that interesting. There was certainly not much focus on business there, nor on the real world! However, I still did relatively well and earned a Master's in one year instead of two. It was hard work though, and, for the first time in my life, I had to fully concentrate on learning and to demonstrate that I was disciplined.

Harvard Business School (HBS) (1968–1972)

I then entered the DBA program of study at HBS in 1968. This period also represented years of hard work and, in all honesty, I barely got through. After my oral doctoral defense, the examination committee's chairperson, Professor Dr. Charles Christenson, said "I guess you have passed"! Professor Richard F. Vancil was my great mentor. He invited me to work on his data-based project on formal planning systems practices. This involved many questionnaires, data coding, and a lot of computer analysis (SPSS). It was a challenge to get the computer-based data analysis done in those early days of computing, with punch cards, paper printouts, and data computing centers. I had to sleep on a camp bed in the data center to be able to get more "runs" done. Professor Vancil "pushed" me in a good way, so that I would go on to complete my doctorate on time (1971). At the end of my doctoral studies at HBS, I was invited for a job interview at Chicago's Graduate School of Business (Booth). I worked feverishly to get my computer-based analysis completed and, in the end, got it all done around midnight, before leaving for Chicago the next morning. I completed my presentation while on the plane! But disappointingly, I did not get the job at Booth.

Key Learnings

What are some of the key learnings from this journey in my upbringing and education? For me, there are two particular points:

* While it may, at first glance, look as if the educational path that I pursued was driven by rather random events, this may de facto not be

1 Upbringing and Education 9

entirely the case. My clear aspiration to pursue a cutting-edge education in business could have had a lot to do with how things came about in the real world. So my educational progress was at least in part driven by my aspirations and *not* solely by random events.

- Hard work seems to be a sine qua non. There is no such thing as a free ride when it comes to this. Dedication and discipline are mandatory. At times, one's plans or ambitions will be frustrated, necessitating an extra input of effort. Hard work is often needed, both when it comes to academia as well as for businesses to succeed. Successfully leading an academic institution, including implementing state-of-the-art curricula, will often mean overcoming frustrations.

These conclusions have clear implications. A meaningful curriculum, for instance, should inspire students to develop their aspirations, to search for new paths, and to break traditional boundaries. A good curriculum should stimulate new thinking, not present the current body of knowledge as "this is it"! This kind of open-ended curriculum is only feasible, of course, when learners are prepared to put in hard work. This is the case universally, both in academia as well as in business.

2

Experiences from Academia and Academic Administration

Academic Posts

IMEDE (1971–1973)

My first academic position was with IMEDE, the executive development institute located in Lausanne, Switzerland. This turned out to be a very productive time for me. I published a lot, both articles and cases, and co-edited a book with Professor Victor Norman of NHH. But I certainly did not fully understand IMEDE's practitioner-orientated teaching culture—managerial and with a heavy focus on quality teaching—and thus I got fired when my contract was up after two years. According to the then head of IMEDE, Mr. Luigi Dusmet, I was "too aloof."

I met Professor Warren McFarland from Harvard Business School (HBS) on the same evening I was let go. He was complimentary about my publications record and seemed to be quite surprised when I told him that I had been fired earlier that day. Dr. McFarland, a specialist in IT, had good contacts at MIT's Sloan School of Management in addition to HBS. Within a few days, I was invited to give job interview presentations both at Sloan and at HBS. I was then offered an Assistant Professorship

© The Author(s), under exclusive license to Springer Nature Switzerland AG 2022
P. Lorange, *Learning and Teaching Business*,
https://doi.org/10.1007/978-3-031-14564-3_2

12 P. Lorange

at Sloan and also a Senior Lectureship position at HBS. I turned down HBS, not wanting to become a "glorified apprentice" at the same academic institution where I had gotten my doctorate less than two years earlier.

MIT's Sloan School of Management (1973–1980)

I accepted the Sloan School's offer and became part of the Management Science group within the Management Control subsector. This was a productive period, with a lot of pressure to "publish or perish," and with exceptionally good students. MIT's culture was eclectic, and I had some great colleagues. Still, I worked mostly alone. In retrospect, I was perhaps too isolated. I was promoted to Associate Professor in 1977, however, but I did *not* get tenure in 1980. Obviously, I was greatly disappointed.

In early 1974, I married Liv Martinsen. I had met Liv two years before, when I was with IMEDE, and we had gone skiing together in Verbier, Switzerland. A fellow Norwegian, she was a purser at Pan American, the later defunct US airline. Initially, we lived in an apartment in Cambridge, MA, and later moved to a home in suburban Weston, MA, in October Lane. Our first child, Per Frithjof, was born in 1974 while still in Cambridge, and our second child, Anne Sophie, was born in 1976 when we resided in Weston. For me, this was a happy time, getting married and becoming the father of two healthy children.

I got divorced from Liv in 1999, however. But I have always maintained close contact with my two children, and this continues to this day. Both children attended the Christian High School in Oslo. Per Frithjof moved on to attend NHH, and then took a master's degree at the University of California Berkeley, and later a doctorate (in Comparative Literature) at the University of Oslo. He is now President of S. Ugelstad Invest (see Chap. 6) and lives in Sandefjord, outside Oslo, with his wife, Kristin, and a daughter, Karen Annine, as well as a son, Hans Andreas. Anne Sophie took her bachelor's degree at BI and a master's degree at the International School of Arts and Artworks. She is now a successful painter and is married to Frode Lervik. They have three daughters, Elise, Madeleine, and Louise, and live in Oslo.

Wharton (1980–1989)

After leaving MIT, I ended up taking a professorial position at the Wharton School, University of Pennsylvania. I was offered tenure immediately, a factor that was part of my decision to move. I was seen as a relatively successful "up and coming" professor and was promoted to full professor in 1983. Key support came from Professor Dr. John Lubin—then department head and chair of the Management Department (Strategy, HR, Labor Relations, Entrepreneurship, and Family Business). I taught mainly within Strategic Planning and Control, primarily using case studies. The Swedish banker and industrialist Jacob Wallenberg, among others, took my planning course. Having bright, talented students throughout my various positions has been rewarding and inspiring to me. I have always enjoyed having a connection with those I taught as well as, at times, learning a great deal from them, either then or later when our paths would cross again. While Wharton seemed to be quite a silo orientated, I did develop good personal relationships with colleagues from Marketing, such as Professors J. Wind and T. Robertson, as well as, in Finance, A. Santamero.

For the family, however, the move to Philadelphia was quite dramatic and abrupt. My wife, Liv, was particularly unhappy in the beginning. We ended up building our own home in Bryn Mawr (Hillhouse Ave.) outside Philadelphia, and we all gradually came to enjoy our nine years there very much. Our children attended the Shipley School in Bryn Mawr. It was a happy time!

Stockholm School of Economics (SSE) (1983–1984)

My primary activity as a visiting scholar at SSE was to give a doctoral seminar on International Business. Each of my students had to make at least three positive contributions at each class session before coming up with any critical comments. I chose this technique to counterbalance the tendency of doctoral students to be overly critical. My small family enjoyed the year in Stockholm, and we lived in an apartment in Ulrikagatan, at Östermalm.

Roles in Academic Administration

MIT's Sloan School of Management

Earlier, while still at Sloan. I was sub-department Head of the Management Control area for around two years. In retrospect, I was probably too young and inexperienced to be effective in this position, however.

Wharton (1985–1990)

I became Head of the Management Department, Wharton's largest, from 1985 to 1988, and also Head of Wharton's International Business Research Center from 1986 to 1988, before becoming Head of the Lauder Institute (a combined offering of MBA and MA; university-wide, reporting to the Provost) from 1988 to 1990.

My wife Liv had a major influence on the decision to leave US academia. I had then narrowly won the election as Head of Norwegian School of Business (BI) in 1989. In my first year, I commuted between Oslo and Philadelphia, while finishing up at Wharton. Needless to say, the decision to leave the United States and move back to Norway was a major one. In retrospect, it turned out to be good to move back to Europe.

Norwegian School of Business (BI) (1989–1993)

The entire family settled in Well, Oslo, where we moved into a newly constructed penthouse apartment in Hoffsveien, on the western side of Oslo. As already mentioned, my two children were then enrolled at Oslo Christian High School.

After I became President at BI (I changed the title from Dean to President), one of my first moves was to ask each faculty member to write down what they considered to be the three most important issues for BI and on their personal agendas, as well as the three least pressing ones. This gave me a good understanding of the key issues I should pursue in my new job. This was subsequently followed up with more systematic faculty reviews leading, in particular, to a relatively stronger focus on research. Some important new faculty appointments were also made.

Building a relationship with Norway's public sector—in particular, the parliament and the ministerial office for education—took a lot of time but led to a stronger recognition of BI's role as the preeminent privately owned academic institution in Norway, including paving the way for BI's takeover of Oslo Business School and Norway's Marketing College. My closest associates were Tove Strand Gerhardsen (see Chap. 4), Björn Berntsen (CFO), and Knut Lange (P.A.).

BI's system of regional schools, a very successful network, was also further strengthened under my management. And we developed new offerings in real estate management and tourism management which were subsequently approved by the public sector.

Finally, important links were developed with Norway's business sector, including the establishment of a successful business–academic executive development network. In 1993, after having initially agreed to run for a second term as President at BI, I was approached by IMD to take over the top position there. This would imply greater interaction with a top-quality faculty and students at a leading European and worldwide academic institution, even though it represented much smaller numbers of staff and students than at BI.

IMD (1993–2008)

The remainder of this chapter discusses my next position as head of IMD as well as my family's move to Lausanne, Switzerland.

The Transition to IMD

How was I nominated as a candidate for the top job at IMD? I recall that I was proposed by the then President of IMD's alumni organization in Norway, Mr. Henrik Wessel, who was relatively influential in the IMD organization, having successfully chaired the annual IMD world alumni conference in Oslo a few years previously. My candidacy was only introduced into the search process at the last minute, however.

I interviewed for the job as President (then Directeur Général) of IMD. We met in a private meeting room at Zurich Airport twice, the first time for me to learn in more detail about the job and their offer, and the second time for me to bring up any last-minute concerns before eventually accepting. In addition to the Chairman of IMD's Foundation Board, Mr. Kaspar Cassani (ex-President, IBM, Switzerland), the Institute's Chief Financial Officer, Mr. Philipp Koehli, and the Chief Administrative Officer, Mr. Robert Toletti (ex-IBM), also attended. Our second meeting, though, ran into some unexpected and surprising problems. I had to change plane in Frankfurt on my journey from Oslo. As we were about to take off from Frankfurt, a bird was sucked into one of the plane's jet engines and the pilot had to return the aircraft to the terminal. Another plane was provided relatively quickly, but all of this took quite a lot of time. In the end, there was barely any time for me to be able to say yes to the job!

When I arrived at IMD, my title as the person in charge was the French "Directeur Général" (IMD is located in the French-speaking part of Switzerland). I immediately informed the board and the faculty that this might be dysfunctional for a school operating globally and suggested the title should be President instead. And so it became! Four years earlier I had spearheaded a similar process at BI, changing my title there from Dean to President.

Not long after I had taken over as President of IMD (1993), I went to the United States, where I revisited Harvard Business School—the institution where, more than two decades earlier, I had spent three years working toward my doctorate (1968–1971). I met with the then Dean of HBS, Dr. John McArthur, a Canadian, from Vancouver, and asked him what advice he might have for me when it came to managing IMD. Incidentally, Dr. McArthur had earlier spent a year as a research associate at IMEDE. He responded, after pausing briefly to think: "show interest in the health of your faculty and their families." At the time, I was very surprised. I think I had expected some deeper strategic insight! But as time went by I came to realize the power of this statement. At IMD, I did indeed initiate a voluntary health coverage program, Preferred Global

Health (PGH), for the Institute's faculty, all paid for by the Institute. This would ensure medical treatment for critical illnesses at the world's most reputable medical institutions. Two of IMD's faculty were later treated for life-threatening diseases through the program. These faculty members were not only very grateful but also became effective "ambassadors" for the program. All IMD's faculty bar one signed up, and the positive effect on faculty morale was high. All of this can be traced back to the advice I had received from John McArthur sometime earlier.

Business Development

One of the key responsibilities of my new role was to manage IMD's nine-person sales force. The Japanese market became my sole responsibility. I made many corporate visits all over the world, accompanied by IMD's marketing executives, who oversaw the various markets. My direct involvement in IMD's revenue generation gave me added credibility, both among IMD's faculty as well as among IMD's Foundation Board members. To this day, I still believe in getting involved, in hands-on doing, in action, in project ownership in the true sense of the word. Someone in a position of power, I believe, should not just observe and oversee but also be on the front line, in the field.

CEOs seem to have respected me, acknowledging that I may perhaps possess some valuable insights into managerial knowledge. My opinions seemed to be generally appreciated, including at IMD's CEO roundtables. Early on during my tenure at IMD, the then Chairman, Dr. Fritz Leutwiler (formally head of Switzerland's National Bank), said "Peter, you have been picked for this job not to be popular, but to get the job done." I was also invited to attend the monthly lunch with all the members of Nestlé's top management team at their headquarters in Vevey. Peter Brabeck, the former CEO of Nestlé, once stated that I may be "one of the best sales persons he might have ever met." My relationship with Nestlé remained strong throughout my 15 years as President of IMD.

There is one incident involving Nestlé that was particularly meaningful to me. I was asked by my initial Chairman, Mr. Cassani, to go to the Nestlé headquarters in Vevey to meet with their then President/CEO,

18   P. Lorange

Mr. Helmut Maucher. He stated "I hope that you will not come back and ask for money to cover possible future losses. I often used to see your predecessors regarding this in years past. *But,* if you truly feel that you are in an economic squeeze, then please come and see me." I never had to go back to him to ask for additional funding. Professor Xavier Gilbert, who also studied for his doctorate at HBS, was acting Director General of IMD in 1983 and, perhaps by necessity, had to focus rather heavily on cost-cutting. It turned out, however, that this might have slowed down future growth. The earlier resignation of Dr. Juan Rada, the first President of IMD, seems to have been influenced by Helmut Maucher (head of Nestlé). He may have viewed Dr. Rada as not being a sufficiently effective leader, as perhaps not being adequately capable of building confidence among IMD professors. Having a brilliant personal intellect is not always enough when it comes to being an effective President. It is perhaps fair to say that IMD was in a state of crisis when I arrived.

Faculty Management

I tried to give faculty and staff members sufficient "freedom" to be entrepreneurial. Two quotes from General Norman Schwarzkopf should be mentioned here, both of which are still meaningful to me:

> "When put in command, take charge!"
> "When in doubt, do the right thing." [1]
> (Schwarzkopf, 1992)

For me, it was also important to stimulate teamwork, rather than having faculty and staff working in silos.

The hiring of new faculty and staff is critical at an institution such as IMD; perhaps this is quite similar to what happens when the manager in charge of a football team recruits new soccer players. There were three key aspects to be checked off when hiring and I embraced these completely:

---

[1] In their recent book, Paul Polman and Andrew Winston give this same quote (Net Positive, 2021), without providing the source, however. Regrettably, most readers might be misled to believe that this quote is theirs!

2 Experiences from Academia and Academic Administration 19

* Does he/she seem to understand (at least most of) the state-of-the-art knowledge requirements of the job?
* Does he/she have an attitude of "giving more than you take," with an aversion to "silos," i.e., "me, me, me."
* Teaching and research are *both* key and both must be mastered.

Reviews of each faculty member's performance were undertaken regularly, every six months, and were based on standardized written reports from each faculty member. Relatively large bonuses were granted to truly top performers.

Succession

There were five Chairmen of IMD's Foundation Board during my 15 years as President: Mr. Caspar Cassani (who recruited me, ex-President, IBM Europe), Dr. Fritz Leutwiler (ex-President, Switzerland's Central Bank), Mr. Vito Baumgartner (ex-President, Caterpillar Europe), Mr. Heini Lippuner (ex-President, Ciba-Geigy), and Dr. Matti Alahuhta (ex-SVP, Nokia, ex-CEO Kone, ex-Head of Finland's Industrial Association).

When it came to picking my successor as President in 2008, Matti, Heini, and I had agreed that Matti would be the preferred candidate. However, Matti withdrew his candidacy at the last minute to become CEO of Kone instead. I was not prepared for this and I had not done much to prepare for the succession of key administrators, particularly a successor to Dr. Jim Ellert (Associate Dean, Faculty) or Mr. Philipp Koehli (CFO). Should that have been done? Or would this be an issue to be decided on by my successor?

A search committee was established to find the new President. The Egon Zehnder search organization supported the committee. Dr. John Walsh, a Practice Professor at Harvard Business School was chosen. But apparently there was not much background checking done. Matti, who was on the committee, told me that he was satisfied that John Walsh had the rank of professor at HBS. But John was only a "practice professor." Matti seemingly did not realize the difference between this and a tenured professor. I was told to stay away from the succession process and instead authored a book on my experiences of running a leading business school. When asked to meet the faculty members elected by the rest of the faculty to be on the search committee (John Walsh, Leif Sjögren, Tom Malnight), I went through some of the leadership principles laid out in the book (Lorange, 2008). However, this was not met with much interest by them.

There were two incidents that I experienced when interacting with John Walsh before he was installed in his new position that sticks particularly in my mind:

* When I met John for the first time, over lunch at Beau Rivage Café, he indicated that he did not plan to work anywhere near as hard as I had done. My sense was that he implicitly felt that there was perhaps an element of "stupidity" in what I had done. My thinking, however, was that one always needs to put in the effort that is required to get a job done in a satisfactory way.
* When having dinner with John Walsh, Jim Ellert, and Philipp Koehli, also at Beau Rivage Café, Philipp was outlining what he saw as some of the key issues associated with his job as CFO and Head of Administration. Dr. Walsh apparently disagreed and abruptly left the table. It should be noted that, at a later stage, Dr. Walsh "sidelined" Philipp Koehli by promoting someone else to take over many of the latter's functions.

The issue of who might be an effective successor as President of IMD was of considerable concern to me, especially from around 2005. For me, it was a matter of personal importance that the school's excellent trajectory should continue. Others had similar thoughts.

Having a strong succession had been a key motivation for me to write down the key dimensions of the job, hoping that this might be beneficial to my successor. This became my book *Thought Leadership Meets Business: How Business Schools Can Become More Successful* (2010). The book was well received in general, but perhaps not quite so well by IMD's new leadership team.

Looking back at my 15 years as President of IMD, I must confess that I had a sense of pride. IMD has undoubtedly evolved in a good way and was indeed considered one of the world's leading business schools by the time I left in 2008. It was thus particularly rewarding for me to be designated as Honorary President many years later, in 2021.

Family Considerations

When I was appointed President of IMD in 1998, my two children were still in high school, and Liv and I did not want to take them out of the Norwegian school system. For the children to shift to the Swiss school system would have been very disruptive. So, while I spent most of my time in Lausanne, the rest of the family remained in Norway, coming to Switzerland for short trips. We initially rented an apartment in Pully, later purchasing a penthouse apartment, also in Pully, on Route de Vevey. After four years, Liv then also moved permanently to Switzerland.

I bought this penthouse apartment in Pully when it was constructed in 1996. I took it as a good sign that the building's own architect, Argentina-born Ignacio Dahl Rocha, also moved into the same building (and still lives there!).

I also bought an apartment in Verbier, around 90 min away from our home in Pully, located very close to Verbier's main ski lifts. I bought it new from the developer, Bjørn Mydske, in 1997. A major reason was to stimulate my family's search for a good outdoor life. A key contact of mine in Verbier is Chris Stackelberger who owns and runs a hotel next door.

I then bought an apartment in Küssnacht am Rigi in 2010, from a neighbor, Beat Egli. It was then new. There were two primary reasons for me deciding to leave Canton Vaud for Canton Schwyz, located on the picturesque banks of the Vierwaldstättersee. The first was to be closer to the bulk of Switzerland's business community, primarily in Zurich, Basel, and Lucerne, having just also purchased a real estate facility in Horgen (around 30 minutes away), which eventually became Lorange Institute. Secondly, there was a somewhat more streamlined cantonal administration in the much smaller Canton Schwyz. This administration struck me as being more business friendly and easier to deal with than that of Canton Vaud. There was also a substantial tax advantage in moving to this canton.

Commandore, the Royal Norwegian Order of Merited Services (2010)

I received this award on September 6th, 2010, for services to Norwegian industry and academia. I had an audience with King Harald V of Norway later that year at Oslo Castle, to thank him for this. This order is given to citizens living outside Norway and is the equivalent of the St. Olav's Order, which is presented to notable citizens living in Norway. I was impressed by the King's intimate knowledge of the work of Professor H.P. L'Orange, a distant relative of mine, who was an art historian, archaeologist, and author, and the first head of the Norwegian Institute in Rome. The King was equally well versed in how the Chinese economy was advancing. He told me that he used to visit China twice a year, incognito.

Hard work has always been a mantra for me. Relatedly, Norway's leading newspaper, *Affenposten*, ran a series where key individuals who hold high positions within society, i.e., with successful careers, were interviewed about what they thought were the most important factors behind their success (*Affenposten*, 10/9/2021, p. 27). Almost all of those interviewed stressed that hard work, drive, and self-determination were critical. But they also stressed the importance of having been supported by others, such as colleagues and bosses. Having been brought up in a supportive home, with hard work as a core value, was also seen as key. But in the end, a degree of good luck was needed. It was seen as important to be ready to grasp a good opportunity when it arose. One of the people interviewed, Mr. Johan H. Andresen, owner of the large investment conglomerate Ferd, also stressed the importance of "giving back," by working with what he calls "social entrepreneurs." His father was one of my board members at BI.

Key Learnings

So, what are some of the key lessons that might be taken from this "journey" through my career in academia and in academic administration, accompanied and supported by my family? I have been thinking a lot about this and have ended up with two conclusions which for me seem

2 Experiences from Academia and Academic Administration 23

particularly important. As one gets older, one has more time to think, to go back in time, to recognize one's mistakes, sorrows as well as joys and successes. I did that, and still do. This is what I call lessons or learnings. As someone dedicated to learning and education, I believe first and foremost that every experience offers an occasion for learning. So, this type of reflection, allowing me to identify specific learnings, has brought me comfort. The first conclusion relates more to my academic career, while the second is more closely linked to my career in academic administration, and also to my all-important family, of course:

- Trying to understand the key cultural features of the academic institution which one has joined seems paramount. At IMEDE, for instance, it was critical to deliver managerially relevant teaching. Research publications, on the other hand, did not seem to be as highly valued. I did not understand this and threw myself into research instead, producing a heavy stream of research outputs. In the end, this resulted in my dismissal. In contrast, at the Sloan School of Management, MIT, research, or "publish or perish," was central, and cooperative research was also seen as key. Here too, I missed out. I spent too much of my efforts on individually driven research and too much time on publishing more general books on strategic planning rather than on articles reporting on my research. In the end, I was denied tenure. At Wharton, however, a combination of research-based publishing and relevant teaching was valued, and there seemed to be greater flexibility as to where one might put one's efforts. I seemed to have a better understanding and, as a result, did relatively well.
- The successful administration of academic institutions seems to depend on the leader's ability to motivate his/her team, i.e., "give more than one takes," with the precondition that the team must also be able to respect the leader. Academic credibility based on a successful track record is also key. Achieving all of this requires harmony within one's family. It will be untenable in the longer run to excel in leadership if there is no harmony at home. One might compare the running of a family with running a business. Both require vision, passion, grit, creativity, and commitment. Fortunately, my ex-wife had all of this in abundance, while I was regrettably falling short.

In conclusion, I believe that an effective academic career should guide learners to acquire a better understanding of the most critical basic values that drive such different institutions.

Further, it is crucial for effective leaders to be able to encourage the members of their institutions to adopt these specific core values. There is probably a strong "spill-over effect" to the leading of businesses also when it comes to this.

3

The Role of Research

I was President of IMD, one of the world's leading business schools, for 15 years, from 1993 to 2008. I said then, "if a business school wants to work with its clients as leading partners, ... [such a] business school depends on a rich stream of research in order to help a client learn how to learn ...seeking, finding, and presenting new management material in a variety of forms is often called the 'research process' and it rests on the school's firm commitment to discovery ...each faculty member, trained through a doctoral program and on the job, to pursue ideas, discover new truths, test material hypotheses, to learn new things". For me, a commitment to research has always been critical, stemming back to my years as a doctoral student at Harvard Business School, and manifested through my early career as a faculty member at MIT's Sloan School of Management, at Wharton School, University of Pennsylvania, and ever since.

Fields of Research

My research has fallen into five different areas. Let me first make a general observation, however. The process of writing is central for me—it helps me to reach a greater clarity. Publishing in top-quality journals can

© The Author(s), under exclusive license to Springer Nature Switzerland AG 2022
P. Lorange, *Learning and Teaching Business*,
https://doi.org/10.1007/978-3-031-14564-3_3

perhaps be seen as some sort of quality assurance, given that one's work is peer reviewed.

There have been at least three overriding factors that have driven my writing (Moore & Sonsino, 2020, pp. 169–181):

* The process of writing leads to a clarification of one's thoughts and learning.
* Drawing upon one's own experiences seems key—i.e., focusing on practical relevance rather than abstract prescriptions.
* Drawing on the data, analyzing, and writing/rewriting, i.e., a process that involves "doing the work for the reader," leads to a clear synthesis.

I will briefly review each of the five topic areas that have constituted my major research interests with short delineations of the main themes. Details of all the books mentioned in this section can be found in the Appendix.

Shipping

The main focus of my work in this area has been on how to develop more effective strategies for shipping firms, as well as innovations in shipping. The books I have written draw on my background as a former owner of S. Ugelstad Rederi (SUR), being an active shipping investor (through Sole, Pareto, Clarkson-Platou, or Rye-Florenz), and, finally, as a board member of several shipping firms (Olsen & Ugelstad, Knud I. Larsen, Royal Caribbean Cruise Lines, Seaspan). Three fundamental principles for success seem to be emerging from my research on shipping:

* The importance of cycles—"in-out/long-short" (see Chap. 15).
* Timing—here too there is a process issue (see Chaps. 13 and 15).
* The key importance of innovation—again, there is a process issue here (see Chap. 14).

All three of these principles should be key, not only as elements of a successful business school and its curriculum, but also for business.

Family Business

My experiences as the owner of SUR and subsequently of S. Ugelstad Invest (SUI) are central to this stream of research. This was summarized in my 2019 book *A Brief History of S. Ugelstad Invest*. SUI has five strategic foci: stocks/bonds, real estate, shipping, ventures, and education. Several principles for developing and managing a family-owned portfolio company are discussed in this book, including the importance of the transition from one generation to the next. My book *Reinventing the Family Firm* (2021) provides a fairly succinct summary of my research in this area. The current book is also meant as a guide for owners and managers active in family business, as well as offering my thoughts on the essential topics required in today's business schools and business.

A key finding of my research in this area is that privately held firms often tend to outperform publicly held firms. There seem to be at least three reasons for this:

- A longer-term time horizon than is often found in publicly traded firms.
- A more streamlined decision-making structure than that of publicly traded firms. Hence, decisions can often be reached more quickly, with relatively less delays generated by members of the management team and/or board.
- An ability to commit relatively large sums to the financing of innovations and R&D. The owners will often see this as a priority, with relatively less focus on delivering steady dividend streams.

Strategic Planning

Effectively controlling for the effective implementation of strategies was the main theme of my doctoral thesis (1973), as well as the focus of my 1986 book with Professors Scott-Morton and Goshal. While strategic control is certainly not the main driver for the development of good strategies, it is nevertheless important for keeping strategies "on track." I like to think there is an analogy between strategic control and navigational steering systems in inter-ballistic rockets!

Coming up with an operational approach to the development of better strategies in multidivisional firms has been a central driver of my research in strategic planning. This process is interactive and iterative—indeed, it is a valuable learning process—and culminates with clear strategic plans. This includes the development of budgets for future strategies. This work complements business operations (as usual). Two of my books, from 1978 (with Vancil) and from 1982, are central here. Significantly, the conceptual scheme for developing strategic plans in divisional firms, initially reported in the book I co-authored with Professor R.F. Vancil in 1977, also seems to work well for many family businesses.

Another book, co-authored with Lorange & Rembiszewski (2016), articulates ways of coming up with a set of deliberate innovations, orchestrated from the top, in order to ameliorate the frequent tendency for businesses to decay. Effective communication is seen as particularly important here.

How should executive development be shaped now that the COVID-19 pandemic is more or less over, i.e., what will the "new normal" look like? My book on this topic (2021) is co-edited with Santiago Iniguez, and features inputs from around 25 world-leading experts. Many of the design issues that should be reflected in effective curricula for leading academic institutions of the future are suggested in much of what is covered in this book.

Strategic alliances are increasingly seen as key to growing one's business, perhaps in the light of the increased prominence of so-called network strategies. This topic is discussed in books I published in 1987 (with Roos), 1988, 1992, and in two books co-edited with Contractor (1988, 2002). The broad evolutionary thinking driving network-driven strategic processes has been captured in two co-edited books (1993, 2000).

Finally, strategic planning processes in family businesses are discussed in Lorange, 2019a, b (pp. 61–63).

Top Line and Bottom Line

Developing viable strategies can often give rise to dilemmas. My book with Chakravarthy & Lorange (2007) discusses how to cope with what is often seen as one such dilemma—whether to focus on profit *or* growth. We argue that both might be achieved simultaneously and that this might not be a conundrum after all. Our research finding contradicts conventional knowledge on this subject. Growth is particularly key for most organizations. This also seems to drive profitability! It is a matter of going for both, at the same time.

This approach was a key pillar for our strategy at IMD during my years as President. Sales more than quadrupled over 15 years. Improvements in profit came along as well. When I started out as IMD's President in 1993, the school was barely breaking even and IMD also had considerable debts. When I left in 2008, there were no debts, but a reserve of more than CHF 100 million in the bank! A key to all of this was to implement a strategy that drew on the so-called "Say's Law" (named after the French economist, Jean-Baptiste Say (1767–1832), which states that "supply creates its own demand," a dictum that contrasts sharply with what most economists believe, namely that "increased demand leads to more supply." At IMD, we introduced new innovative program offerings which, in turn, led to more demand! The school's "Orchestrating Winning Performance" program (OWP), for instance, attracted more than 800 students per annum as early as four years after it had been introduced. An important corollary from this research is that a joint focus on the long term and the short term is essential, i.e., "today for today, as well as today for tomorrow." Going exclusively for profits, i.e., taking a short-term view, is often not viable in the long term. This is something that business leaders should reflect on when they place a strong emphasis on quarterly financial results.

Educational

This research stream focuses on what might be labelled "The Business School of the Future." My experiences as President of both Norwegian School of Business (BI), (Oslo) and IMD (Lausanne), as well as my experience in building Lorange Institute and later Lorange Network, are central here. Greater speed and flexibility, blended learning (in auditoriums and/or distance-based), and less extensive delivery costs (lower professorial salaries; smaller physical campuses) are key. Books that I authored in 2002, 2005, and 2013 (with Thomas and Sheth) and 2019 are central here.

A key driver for this line of investigation is how to come up with more effective forms of advanced academic teaching. This seems to be related to coming up with more cost-efficient forms of institutions of higher learning. This has been a key driver for the reflections made in the current book, which are summarized in Chap. 16, Learning in the Future: Individuals, Business and Academic Institutions, which discusses better curriculum design for leading academic institutions.

Hence, as I will go on to discuss in Chap. 5, after stepping down from the leadership of IMD in 2008, I set out to embark on two real-life "experiments," to try to come up with more cost-effective forms for institutions of higher learning, Lorange Institute, and Lorange Network.

A particularly important lesson from this is that you "learn as you go"! While IMD, for instance, was a highly efficient institution, I felt that the costs of delivery were simply too high. This then became a major driver for me to launch Lorange Institute. But, as time went by, and I realized that significant cost savings were indeed possible, there were still limitations to this business model—above all, a lack of ability to upscale, with the classroom as the bottleneck! For this reason, I went on to establish Lorange Network. I was able to see that even more cost savings could be had.

While the key benefits seem clear, particularly due to scalability, I am convinced that further "experiments" need to be made in the future to come up with even more efficient designs for institutions of higher learning. But this will be up to others! My sense, however, is that a further search for innovations will probably have to focus relatively heavily on real-world needs in order to be useful. Let it also be said that these conclusions might equally apply when it comes to business organizations.

Key Learnings

Research is certainly the driving force for many aspects of academia and business alike. For me, the question of how to come up with effective new business models for well-performing academic institutions is of particular interest. One key aspect of this, curriculum design, will be discussed in Chap. 16. Research provides a stimulus for we humans to see things clearer, so that we can understand things better and, in the end, make better decisions. Coming up with appropriate designs to inspire the quality of learning in leading academic institutions has always been central for me. Hence, for me, this has meant a lot of research on this topic. This is what this book is all about.

4

Influences from Family and Friends

In this chapter, I will reflect on influences from family and nonfamily members.

Influences from Family Members

I will start with my father (Per Lorange—1916–2002). While there are many positive associations that come to mind when I think about my late father, five particular things stand out for me. My father held a strong belief in technology. He saw this as a panacea for tackling many of life's challenges and problems. While a total belief in the virtues of technology might be perhaps taking things a little too far, there is definitely an important insight here. Technology is important; disciplinary thinking seems key. And being able to anticipate technological advances is critical.

My father also always emphasized the importance of being well prepared, which is perhaps best exemplified by his many successes in ocean racing, including the attention paid to the maintenance of his two sailboats, where all equipment, including sails, was always in superb order. He further placed great store in being fair, which included treating all his

© The Author(s), under exclusive license to Springer Nature Switzerland AG 2022
P. Lorange, *Learning and Teaching Business*,
https://doi.org/10.1007/978-3-031-14564-3_4

three children equally. This also clearly dominated his thinking when it came to giving up his preferential rights to the Store Stabekk farm at Hövik near Oslo: as the oldest son, he decided not to take over his parents' farm, but rather to pass the running of the firm on to his younger brother. Incidentally, this action later motivated me to give up *my* rights, as my father's oldest son, so that all six grandchildren (my two sisters, three cousins, and myself) might be treated equally. My father also gave me good advice on how to behave at social gatherings, saying "let others talk – they typically enjoy having their own voices heard!" I have often experienced the truth of this advice. My good friend Bjørg echoes this approach, stressing that giving others plenty of opportunities to speak up not only makes them feel good, but that it is also a matter of courtesy. Importantly, a domineering conversational profile might be experienced as signaling a lack of interest in the other party, and perhaps even arrogance.

My father always stressed the value of education as something that can "never be taken away from an individual." Wealth might be lost, but competence through education would always remain with an individual. For him, it was therefore key for my sisters and I to get a good education. My father "lived" this principle to the extreme himself. He was very proud of being certified as an auto-mechanic, in addition to being a prominent civil engineer. He felt that this would always be something to fall back on in the event of a crisis.

Allow me now to make a few reflections about my late mother (Elisabeth, 1917–2007). She was always positive, inclusive, and warm. She was both unassuming and hardworking and always showed an interest in others, listening and being supportive. These qualities were manifested in her support of a wide array of philanthropic organizations. She always looked for positive solutions to problems, searching for a "win-win." Bjørnsson's expression, "good deeds save our world" (Bjørnsson, 1992), might be a good way of capturing what she stood for. She took a great interest in the arts, particularly in music, theatre, and, of course, literature. This strong artistic curiosity was with her throughout her life, and she also stimulated my own interest in art, probably sparking my resolve to become an art collector.

4 Influences from Family and Friends 35

She also believed that one should always be able to rely on the support of one's parents. Parents should almost always support their children and do what is best for them. She put this into practice, giving selfless support not only to me but also to my two sisters. This left a strong impression on me, and I have tried to put this into practice in my own relationship with *my* two children.

As already noted, my parents were happy to pay for my education, which (including at Norwegian School of Economics and Business Administration (NHH), Yale, and Harvard Business School (HBS)) was initially paid for by them. However, toward the end of my doctoral studies at HBS, I received a relatively large fellowship from the Ford Foundation. In the end, all my studies in the United States (Yale, HBS) ended up being paid for by various stipends (tuition, room/board, travel). But I had no financial worries and felt that I took little to no risks. I had a small amount of savings, initially from my grandparents, and received a modest travel stipend as well. This helped!

I believe it is possible to draw some important lessons for business and for business schools when it comes to these two sides of my mother's personality, having only become clear to me much later on. While much of what needs to be taught today tends to be "factual" and concrete, one should not overlook the fact that warmth is also important for effective learning. Humanism, with its focus on human warmth, is probably more critical than we think. So, which qualities did I acquire from my mother? I would say these include positivity, creativity, altruism, and commitment. Thus, my parents' personalities and impact on me have balanced each other out very well!

Let me now share some further insights about my late ex-wife, Liv (1942–2020). We were married in 1974 and were divorced in 2001. Liv was no doubt frustrated with my being away from home so much, especially during the time I was President of IMD. Over time, she and I came to have different views on how to strike a balance between our professional and private lives, perhaps. For me, it was "work, work, work," including consulting and business activities. I felt that I did this both, not only to enhance my career but also as well to maintain a good standard of living for the family. Liv, however, always suggested that I should be at home more. Liv's life revolved around her family—the two children, in particular. For instance, it was primarily her concern about what would ultimately be best for the children that led our small family to leave the United States in 1990 and move to Oslo. In retrospect, it turned out that she was right! She was always open and positive, with a good outlook on life, and she was non-judgmental. She found it easy to get on with other people. Social gatherings were always a success with her around! She was always elegant, which made her stand out in a crowd. Liv was a great homemaker. Our homes in Cambridge and Weston (MA), Bryn Mawr (PA), Oslo, and Pully (Switzerland) were always kept in impeccable order. And she was a perfect host. Her cooking skills were widely appreciated.

I should also like to highlight a few factors that I very much appreciate when it comes to my two children, Anne Sophie and Per Frithjof. Both of my children are hardworking. They have shown commitment and discipline when it comes to their educational pursuits, both earning their bachelor's degrees in business, Per Frithjof from NHH and Anne Sophie from BI. My son has worked closely with me on business matters for more than 30 years, first on S. Ugelstad's Rederi, and later at S. Ugelstad Invest. He is now President of the latter. He handles responsibility very well, especially when it comes to business timing. My daughter has also demonstrated that she has an unusually strong drive. On top of running her household, with three demanding young daughters, she has become an accomplished artist in the field of abstract painting. She now plays a significant role in the management of my art collection.

Above all, my two children have demonstrated to me the importance of these two challenges:

* Proper timing, both in terms of "getting in" (i.e., investing in business, as well as in art) when certain assets are priced relatively low, and taking profits by "getting out" when assets have (hopefully) increased in value. They seem to be particularly talented at the selling stage of such investments, endeavoring to lock in profits that are sufficient to cover SUI's initial costs, while allowing SUI to benefit from future growth in value of the remainder of such holdings, i.e., "free tickets," and to make new investments in business as well as in art.
* Managing risk, including avoiding getting involved in projects or arts schemes which are too risky (Pabrai, 2007). They place a strong

emphasis on due diligence, particularly when it comes to assessing the track record of the promoters of projects as well as of artists. They are also attempting to stay away from investments that are simply too large and from most (early) start-ups, or many upcoming artists, which often lack revenue-generating track records or which simply do not appreciate. They both have good networks of personal advisors. It is important to me that our family business and my art collection stay in our family for a long time. Stewardship is key (Jaffe, 2020). Avoiding major mistakes is paramount. As always, a key challenge is to find projects, and works of art, with exceptionally low risk by buying at the bottom of certain business cycles and perhaps exiting later on, close to the top of the business cycle, obtaining significant additional value if things work out, thereby ameliorating high uncertainty.

While I have not coached my children explicitly, I have certainly always tried to be supportive. My children and I talk about art and business quite a lot!

My daughter-in-law (Kristin) and son-in-law (Frode) have also taught me many useful life lessons. Kristin is particularly well organized, as reflected in the great way she keeps her home and garden, as well as caring for the children. For me, this is indeed an important learning. Frode is actively involved in SUI, particularly when it comes to providing useful inputs to the group's investment strategy. He is also a member of SUI's investment committee. Frode is thorough and follows up on important matters promptly, including technological issues relating to Lorange Network, as well as the key issues related to the integration of Lorange Network into IMD. This underscores again the importance of being well organized and following up in good time.

I am also close to my two younger sisters, Helene and Anne, and they have had a considerable influence on me. Helene, a successful interior designer, is systematic as well as creative. She is hardworking and disciplined. She and her husband enjoy a large social circle. Helene has always had good connections in the world of the arts and has often given me valuable advice when I have sought to purchase works of art. Anne has had a long, distinguished career in the city of Oslo's school system, including having been both a successful headmistress as well as co-head of Oslo's entire school system. Anne has a broad range of interests in addition to her job, including nature, arts, travel, and literature. And she is practical and handy! My sisters and I jointly own properties Ulvøsund, a summer house outside of Lillesand, and Salmeli, a mountain farm and hunting terrain in southern Norway. There have never been any conflicts between the three of us as co-owners. Rather, this jointly owned set of properties has had a positive effect by fostering regular contact between all three of us. For my sister Helene, living in Denmark, and for me, living in Switzerland, this point of contact with Norway is particularly important. And my two sisters and I enjoy often celebrating Christmas together. We have a good sibling balance!

My brother-in-law, Jens Christian is a successful Danish businessman, having held leading positions in retail, digital payment systems, and as head of a large investment fund. Being a successful investor has, of course, always been important to him. One can always rely on Jens Christian. He is a doer, and he gets on with things! He is always a very positive person, who clearly "gives more than he takes." I appreciate him a great deal.

My grandchildren are still young, I love all five of my grandchildren dearly. Beyond this, there is perhaps not much that might be said just yet in terms of what I might learn from each of them. But a few comments about each of them is merited. They are organized according to their age, in descending order:

* Elise seems to be quite a shy young lady, and she knows her mind! She has a heart of gold.
* Madeleine is a quick learner and is particularly interested in mathematics. And she not only seems to thrive in her schoolwork, enjoying scholastic challenges, but is also quite entrepreneurial, and indeed social.
* Louise is a very outgoing young lady, and always seems to be in high spirits, being very sociable and popular among her friends. She enjoys sports.
* Karen Annine is a highly energetic young girl, a quick learner, and always happy.
* Hans Andreas is the youngest. It is too early to make many further comments about his personality, except that he seems to be exceptionally well-humored, calm, and attentive.

I will not go into detail about the influence that my grandparents had on me, except to stress that they were all hardworking and disciplined people, with a strong "protestant ethic" mode (Weber, 1905). All four of them were very generous! One of my grandparents, Rudolf Ugelstad, had perhaps a stronger impact on me than the other three. Entrepreneurship and business acumen were key here! He seemed to show a strong interest in me, something I have always been thankful for. We had many conversations, some about the "olden days" in Brevik, his birthplace, and many about business as well. His stories of being a successful shipowner, developing his own firm, showed me how important good entrepreneurship was.

Let me round off my reflections on the influence of various family members by highlighting some of the key inputs of some of my eight cousins. Kirsten Frederiksen has a very positive outlook, as does her husband Frithjof. They have become particularly close to me in recent years, since they reside in Pully, only 15 min away from where I now live. Our many lunch and dinner discussions have become highlights for me. The Frederiksens are particularly well abreast of Norwegian affairs and give me welcome updates. Rudolf Ugelstad, Kirsten's brother is also one of my best friends. I was the best man at his wedding. He also often supported me, say, in Finn dinghy sailing, and when we made joint trips with our sailboats on trailers across Europe. In recent years, we have spent some great weekends together, enjoying good wine, food, and insightful conversations, joined by his wife, Janike, an art historian specializing in portrait painting.

Influences from Friends and Colleagues

Let us now change focus slightly and consider key influences that I have gotten from nonfamily members. Clearly, there are many more than mentioned here, and I might obviously also have been able to say more about each of the ones I do mention.

Professor Axel Sømme taught economic geography at NHH. His research and teaching dealt to a large extent with issues that might today fall into the field of corporate strategy. Dr. Sømme was open-minded and had an inspirational personality. He was clearly listening to his students! As noted, he took a strong interest in me. I am indeed grateful to him for developing my interest in academic studies.

Professor Richard F. Vancil of Harvard Business School was my main advisor for my doctoral thesis at HBS (*Behavioral Factors in Capital Budgeting*). Inspiring and competent in many ways (researcher, teacher, consultant, friend), he provided constant and wise inputs into my doctoral research project and was always available for feedback and discussion. Without his constant care and his confidence in me, I do not think that I would ever have been able to finish my doctorate on time, perhaps never at all! His discipline and willingness to work hard inspired me a lot.

Jerry Wind was the Lauder Professor of Marketing at Wharton, a truly accomplished researcher and a great teacher. But, above all, he was keenly interested in pushing *innovations* in academia. From him, I came to understand that high-performing institutions are not only built on outstanding faculty research but also and perhaps equally on the academic institution's ability to stimulate innovations. Jerry demonstrated this many times at Wharton, including in the design of Wharton's executive MBA program, the design and implementation of the University of Pennsylvania's Lauder program (with a joint MBA from Wharton *and* an MA in one of eight languages from the University of Pennsylvania's School of Arts and Sciences), and the launch of Wharton's publishing arm (Wharton Academic Press), to mention just a few of the innovations he spearheaded.

When I took over as President of the Norwegian School of Business (BI) in Oslo, I soon realized that running a privately-owned academic entity in a country that was dominated by government-owned educational institutions represented a special challenge. Relatively close coordination with Norway's public sector was required. I was able to attract Tove Strand as my right-hand person. She came from the left of the country's political spectrum and had been a member of Norway's left-wing cabinet. She stressed the importance of so-called "meeting places," where contacts drawn from various areas of expertise might come together— business *and* academia, private *and* public sectors, left *and* right side of the political spectrum, and so on. This turned out to be a very successful

4 Influences from Family and Friends 41

approach. The principle of openness and inclusiveness was powerful, allowing for complementary ways of seeing things. My learning from this is that effective meeting places are key, with a focus on inclusiveness! Listening, being open-minded, showing interest and not being dogmatic are central elements of this philosophy. This also benefitted my approach to leadership later on, at IMD.

Jim Ellert was the senior associate Dean in charge of faculty at IMD and was my right-hand colleague for more than a decade. A professor of finance, with a PhD from the University of Chicago, he was a gifted teacher and enjoyed universal respect among IMD's faculty. He always took a balanced view, had an evenhanded way of handling issues, and always attempted to come up with fair solutions. What did I learn from Jim? To always attempt to find solutions that all parties can live with, i.e., to search for "win-win." This is in sharp contrast to "agreeing with the last person who happened to be in one's office," and/or to side with one party for "political" reasons. Building up a leadership profile based on fairness and evenness seems paramount. When in doubt, strive for decisions that are best for the institution. Most stakeholders will agree with this in the end!

Bala Chakravarthy has been my main academic collaborator and is also a close friend. Bala and I collaborated on several projects which resulted in two co-authored books and several co-authored articles. Bala was always easy to work with. I have never met anyone with a sharper mind. As is so often the case with outstanding academicians, research and teaching seemed to be naturally complementary for him. Both were executed brilliantly. He is one of the most insightful persons I have met, combining original thinking and cutting-edge managerial experience. Excellence and open-mindedness go together!

Karin Mugnaini, formerly President/COO of Lorange Network, has a keen understanding of several key aspects of operating in a network. I had never before had the privilege of working with such a fast and highly intelligent individual who also has an incredible work ethic and discipline. She is always in good mood. Without her strong involvement, it seems clear that Lorange Network would never have been a success.

42 . P. Lorange

My good friend Bjørg Kibsgaard-Peterson is successful in the real estate business. Highly disciplined, she lives in Nyon. She is also a keen project "addict," always looking for ways to improve on the properties she buys. In addition to valuing her friendliness and intellect, I much appreciate her honesty and directness. She never hesitates to say things the way they are. Her commonsense, coupled with a keen ability to observe, are essential qualities. Of course, it is also great that she always seems to have a positive attitude, is always in a good mood, and even enjoys a glass of wine in my company. In moderation, of course! Telling things the way they are, with no unnecessary "wrapping," is a key learning!

Ebba Wachtmeister was a Swedish countess, who lived in France. She was a horse fanatic. What did I find so attractive about her? Above all, she was such a warm person; I felt that she genuinely cared deeply for me, and this was indeed mutual. Her untimely death from cancer in 2008 was a great loss and a major shock to me. From Ebba, I learned that care, compassion, and loyalty are all, in essence, the same.

Birgitte Holter was born in Sarpsberg, Norway, and attended the Norwegian School of Economics and Business Administration (NHH). She has now joined Yara, the spinoff from Norsk Hydro, working on CO_2 emission issues associated with the firm's fertilizer production. Over the years, we have had many inspiring discussions over our regular dinners. Birgitte has taught me that that environmental initiatives might often be seen to be of significant value to a coalition of stakeholders, so that there is a willingness to pay for these initiatives.

I met Paul Eckbo for the first time in 1974 when he was a doctoral student at Sloan School, MIT, and I was an assistant professor. He impressed me then with his ability to come up with creative solutions to complex problems, and with his willingness to launch business start-ups; an entrepreneurial spirit at its best. He would never give up! One of his ventures, Marsoft, allowed me to develop a better understanding of the underlying research methodology for analyzing cycles in shipping. This probably had a major impact on my understanding of the importance of cycles and of timing. Paul has demonstrated to me the importance of creativity, with speed, risk-willingness, and drive in entrepreneurial activities.

Jens Petter Trangrud has been one of my best friends ever since we both attended high school together in Asker in the early 1960s. A master carpenter and an engineer, Jens Petter has always impressed me with his practical skills. For him, it seems particularly important that solutions are found that might actually work! Jens Petter is also an ardent yachtsman. For ten years, he was a crew member of my father's sailboats. In this role, he demonstrated that effective teamwork must be based on the execution of the tasks at hand, avoiding any "prima donna"-like tendencies or personal acrimony. For me, it was truly inspirational to be a member of this sailing crew, with a "we, we, we" philosophy!

Key Learnings

Most of the takeaway lessons from each of the various stories reported in this chapter would be hopefully more or less self-evident. So, once again, I will merely highlight four issues that are particularly important for me:

* All the family and nonfamily individuals stand out as representing something *unique*, something *critical*. And each individual seems to have a vital quality of authenticity. These unique individuals have made all the difference in my life. But, as I have discovered, it is about more than being gifted. Hard work, commitment, and discipline are equally important!
* Respecting inputs from others and being open-minded play a major role in one's personal and professional development. Many of us have fixed ideas, and it is often hard to modify our viewpoints. Regrettably, this type of rigidity is the antithesis of learning. Having an open mind does not mean that "wishy-washiness" is ok. Firmness, i.e., being steadfast, is essential. This is not the same as rigidity, of course. All the persons discussed in the previous pages were "open-minded."
* Setting a good example that positively impacts on the younger generations is key. For instance, entrepreneurship was a key learning for me, above all handed down from my grandfather. And being willing to share fairly and with good grace is another quality I have learned from several of my family members in particular.

44   P. Lorange

* Sticking together seems to be particularly important, above all for a family. Everyone is different, of course, but we all have strengths and weaknesses that complement each other. Together, they help us all to become stronger. Appreciating each other's qualities is key. Respecting diversity is essential for achieving good business performance, perhaps now more than ever, with the increased prominence of so-called networked organizations.

A combination of these basic values should be reflected in good business practices and in effective business schools as well. This underpinning will support leaders in business as well as in academia in developing their own career paths with ambition and integrity.

Part II
The Influence of Business

This part details key influences that derive from experiences I have gotten through a diverse set of business activities in which I have been involved. Partly, this activity involves entrepreneurial start-ups in the business education sector, where I have strived to come up with more cost-effective ways to carry out business learning, and, partly, from more conventional ship-owning activities as well as in portfolio-based family businesses. My activities as a board member as well as a consultant constitute the third source of business influences.

A key learning for me has been that this diversity of influences seems critical. In contrast, drawing on a narrower source of influences seems to be relatively less productive. Eclecticism is key here! This view contrasts with those of several important authors and thinkers. For many, a strong sense of focus seems to be key (Young, 2012). But what about positive eclectic inspirations then? Perhaps the following quote by Young expresses the essence of this alternative way of learning: "By focusing your learning, it's easier to push forward even when projects get difficult because you've committed yourself to not working on something else until you complete it... The simple case for focused learning is the same reason you focus

46   The Influence of Business

with anything—to avoid crowding your attention with things that are easier to do, but less important". David Allen also stresses the importance of focus, stating that focus creates ideas and thought patterns that may not otherwise occur (Allen, 2011). My own views on this will be discussed in the following chapters.

5

Lorange Institute and Lorange Network

Lorange Institute (2012–2017)

Even though IMD had enjoyed considerable success during most of the 15-year period during which I was President, I was nevertheless searching for even better, alternative ways to "organize" leading business education institutions, the idea being to maintain a similarly high academic level as that of IMD and other leading business schools while reducing the costs. It is perhaps in my character to always aim higher, try to do better, and achieve more! Even after a prestigious spell leading a successful academic establishment, I knew that I could push the envelope in executive education, or at least that I should try. In order to experiment with this—i.e., to try to find more efficient ways for leading business schools to operate and to deliver to the student/client to solve their learning problems—I purchased the former Graduate School of Business Administration (GSBA) school campus located in Horgen, on the shore of Lake Zurich, from Dr. Albert Stähli. This became the Lorange Institute (LI). I developed a new faculty concept based on a stable network of leading professors from other organizational entities, all now being freelance. The idea was to be able to slash faculty costs by only paying for the time when

© The Author(s), under exclusive license to Springer Nature Switzerland AG 2022
P. Lorange, *Learning and Teaching Business*,
https://doi.org/10.1007/978-3-031-14564-3_5

47

faculty members were actually actively teaching. Further, there were three apartments on the LI campus that could be used to accommodate visiting faculty members. Meals could be taken at a restaurant, which was also on campus. The professors came from a wide variety of backgrounds—business schools, consultants, retired executives, and so on. What mattered above all was that they all possessed cutting-edge knowledge within their particular fields of expertise. The curriculum consisted of several modules that could be taken in any sequence leading up to the MBA degree. In addition to the degree program, LI also offered tailored on campus programs for specific firms.

I also put considerable emphasis on the students becoming involved with so-called "living cases." These consisted of group projects where the students would work on real problems that various corporations might have. The course concluded with the writing of a report as well as a presentation to the rest of the class, which was attended by senior executives from the firm that had been the subject of analysis. There tended to be lively "discussion and answer" sessions after these presentations in which the firms' executives also participated. Every student was expected to participate in at least one living case project. I appreciated the fact that we "brought reality into the classroom" so to speak, where the topics were real world, relevant, and actual.

Our pedagogical approach to teaching was also generally quite unconventional. Classes mostly took place in so-called flat-floor classrooms, with students sitting face-to-face around small tables. And the sessions in the classroom were typically rather long, perhaps several hours each. The typical class size would be relatively small, say, no more than 30. The professor's main role was to stimulate debates around topics covered on a specific day which the students would have prepared for beforehand through background readings. Professors were seen more as catalysts rather than as traditional lecturers. In taking this approach, I aimed to stimulate more in-depth learning based on the more active involvement of all.

We also created an advisory board consisting of around 20 senior executives chaired by Mr. Max Amstutz, former CEO of Holcim, which ensured that LI's focus remained relevant and that the Institute's management practices were of a high standard. The advisory council typically met twice a year for half a day and provided a source of general support for the academic direction-setting as well as for the marketing of the Institute's offerings.

But running LI was more difficult than I had anticipated, and things fundamentally did not develop as expected. While being able to significantly reduce costs, LI was never able to gain a sufficient business volume to break even, i.e., to attract enough students for the MBA programs or to offer enough in-company programs. This was, at least in part, due to its inability to gain accreditation from AACSB (Florida) or EFMD (Brussels), two of the world's leading accreditation institutions. LI was only able to get accreditation from AMBA (London). There seemed to be a lack of appreciation for the radically new business model that Lorange Institute represented, particularly as it had no permanent academic staff and "only" a stable network of freelance professors. The main sticking point for the accreditation bodies was that there was no institute-driven research. At LI, each professor was expected to have engaged in relevant research on their own.

So, in 2017, I sold LI to a leading Chinese business school, CEIBS, in Shanghai. CEIBS had been looking for a campus facility in Europe, primarily to provide international exposure for its students, most of whom were Chinese. They also had their own pedagogical approaches. Thus, following the sale, most of LI's teaching methodologies were abandoned. Financially, the sale to CEIBS more than covered my original investment, largely because of a significant appreciation in the value of the land. A further factor was the fact that I had been able to purchase the neighboring building and land from the municipality of Horgen, an old waterworks facility. The combined sales price to CEIBS was thus very satisfactory.

Evaluating the LI project in retrospect, was it a success or not? Was it worth putting in such a considerable amount of effort along with significant financial resources? Yes *and* no. While it became clear that high-quality business school offerings definitely could be delivered in a rather unconventional way, with considerably lower costs than are typically the norm, and that the sale price that was obtained provided satisfactory financial returns, it should also be said that LI was never able to operate on a break-even basis, despite the rather efficient way in which the place was run. I often wonder whether LI was simply too "avant-garde." Or whether I am being overly self-critical. Was it just an ambition of mine to push the educational envelope, rather than identifying a more realistic market problem reflecting a true customer need?

Lorange Network (2017–2021)

However, my experience with LI did not deter me in my efforts to come up with better ways to learn and better ways to exchange knowledge. In fact, it led to a decision to continue to search for a better concept for "the business school of the future." The Lorange Network (LN) was launched in 2017. This would be heavily based on digital technology, namely in the form of a custom-built digital platform, so as to be able to achieve a more realistic scale than we were able to achieve at LI, where the relatively small class sizes were a limiting factor. Further, the intention was to make the curricular offerings so dramatically different from established norms that no accreditation would be needed. Finally, there would be no fixed investment in a campus, since all participants would be studying from their homes and workplaces and interacting with each other onscreen.

LN was advised during the initial strategy period by a leading consultant, Dr. Knut Haanaes from Boston Consulting Group. He stressed that a realistic geographic rollout might *first* take place in Switzerland, a tough and generally rather skeptical market), followed by Germany, also a tough market, but much larger, for then to finally focus on Scandinavia, for me a relatively easy market, being Norwegian and well-known. The rest of the world would then follow later. The client group to be focused on would primarily be leaders of family-owned firms, independent investors, as well as those leading family offices. Executives from publicly owned firms, which are often large, were not included in the target group, other than senior executives who might also have significant personal wealth to manage and hence fall into the target group this way.

As can be seen, the primary target group for LN differs significantly from the one we focused on at LI. The aim was to serve individuals who might more readily appreciate the need to keep themselves updated, unlike (generally) younger students who primarily want to have an MBA on their résumés, not the least to enhance their careers. And we felt that the self-motivation to take lifelong learning seriously might be particularly strong among individuals whose intention was to preserve and further build wealth and those whose current activities or future investments were growth oriented.

There were four classes of offerings:

* Short exposés or insights written by experts, book reviews, and executive interviews. This would provide network members with an efficient way of staying up to date. All the experts were initially recruited by me. I also provided most of the book reviews. A focus on emerging, current themes was the norm.
* Webinars (including Roundtables, Special Presentations, Investor get-togethers), podcasts, and videos of leading executives. This offering has turned out to be very successful and seems to have been well appreciated by LN's 3300 members. The webinar format is typically as follows. We have one main speaker or a small number of panel experts, usually three, to comment on a small set of questions sent out beforehand (usually five questions). Each webinar is limited to one hour in length (with a larger panel, it sometimes extends to 90 min), and there tend to be around 75–100 members participating, all logging in via Zoom. The questions to the panel are then posed by me, acting as moderator. After each webinar, I provide a brief summary, which is then posted on LN's platform. There is typically a minimum of two such webinars per month.
* Deal Wall. This is used by LN to try to match members of the network who have new projects and seek investors with other network members who are looking to invest. There are additional digital sessions, namely Investor get-togethers, separate from those described above, to enhance the "matching" process. These sessions are moderated by my son, Per Frithjof Lorange. Network members who are looking for funding for the projects they are starting present the gist of these business concepts through a sort of live pitch deck with a question and answer period. Typically, three to four projects are presented per online get-together, and there tend to be around 25 network members logged in who are potential investors. Obviously, investors direct their ques-

tions to the founder or other anchor investor so as to increase their own understanding of the projects and, if they are still interested in investing, they can have further dialogue.

* Short educational programs, primarily for family business entrepreneurs and leaders of family firms. These short programs are still being developed. Four were successfully run in 2019 with media giant *The Financial Times* and their joint venture learning company, Headspring. The intention for any future offerings is that they should be modular and fully virtual, drawing to a considerable extent on the relatively large body of materials already developed (book reviews, reports, webcasts, and so on).

LN has undisputedly enjoyed significant success, especially when it comes to the overall membership growth (3300 members), as well as the broad acceptance of the quality and relevance of LN's webinars, podcasts, and interviews. Much of the running of LN's activities were carried out by Ms. Karin Mugnaini, the President and Chief Operating Officer (COO) of LN. I served as the Chairman and CEO. Per F. Lorange was the Head of Deal Wall and Frode Lervik was the CFO. Further support was provided by Elizabeth Schwelger-Ellis. The accounting and tax affairs were managed by a Zurich-based digital bookkeeping firm, in line with the digital philosophy and set-up at LN. A group of IT specialists who ran the various web support functions and programmers were based in Russia.

In mid-2021, it was decided to let IMD take over LN's functions. The major driver for this decision was to secure continuity and expansion in the delivery of the various activities being provided by LN in light of my relatively advanced age (78). LN's activities were taken over by various entities within IMD's organization as of fall 2021.

Key Learnings

What are some of the key learnings from my experiences with Lorange Institute and with Lorange Network, as reported in this chapter? Three factors stand out in particular:

5 Lorange Institute and Lorange Network 53

- A determined search for how to do things better is key—better products and/or services, and at a lower cost. In the end, it is crucial to develop a concept that can be clearly seen to have a favorable benefits/costs ratio that benefits one's target customers! In the end, it is the customer who pays. Happy customers are everything!
- So-called subscription-based business seems to have a lot of advantages, above all in making it easier to maintain some sort of customer base at a reasonable cost, as we saw when it came to Lorange Network. And the stronger one's network gets, the more successful one's business is likely to be. It is a matter of investing time, energy, and hard work, and not just capital. But developing a successful network strategy will typically require ample funding too!
- A clear long-term purpose is key. In a family firm, it is perhaps particularly important to strive for such continuity. In this connection, it is particularly critical to involve the next generation at an early stage, perhaps by transferring formal ownership in a family firm earlier rather than later.

In the next two chapters, I will look at other business activities in which I have been involved. Chapter 6 considers S. Ugelstad's Rederi (heritage business), S. Ugelstad Invest (business portfolio), and other family-related activities. Chapter 7 deals with consulting and board assignments.

6

Family Business Strategies

In this chapter, I will look at three different sets of business activities: S. Ugelstad's Rederi (SUR), a so-called heritage business; S. Ugelstad Invest (SUI), which is a business portfolio activity; and, finally, other family-related activities. The first two of these have been of particular relevance to me. They have also required a heavy input of my time and energy.

This chapter relates to the rest of the book in an important way. While the evolutionary experiences of the business activities described in the following pages will definitely not be seen as always positive, there are nevertheless sufficient examples of "good business practices."

S. Ugelstad Rederi (SUR)

SUR was an Oslo-based ship-owning firm, established in 1929 and run from then until 1939 by Mr. Samuel Ugelstad (1888–1907) and then run by his son, Sam, a cousin of my mother from 1939 to 1988. I inherited 49.9% of the firm in 1991 when he passed away. Then, over a period of six years, I was able to take over full control and, in the end, had 100%

© The Author(s), under exclusive license to Springer Nature Switzerland AG 2022
P. Lorange, *Learning and Teaching Business*,
https://doi.org/10.1007/978-3-031-14564-3_6

55

ownership! The initial inheritance might partly have had to do with how Sam Ugelstad regarded me. This is not based on hard facts, however, and the following might therefore not be much more than guesswork.

I had quite a lot of interaction with Sam Ugelstad and, at times, with his wife Liz, who supported him in running the company. For instance, we had dinner in Hong Kong, and several meetings over the years on his sailboat, (12m, *Lakmée*). We enjoyed a number of dinners at 2nd Etage, Restaurant Hotel Continental, Oslo, and so on. My sense is that Sam Ugelstad developed some degree of trust in me, and that he perhaps appreciated what he might have seen as some professional competences. I was a professor at Wharton by then, and had my doctoral degree from Harvard Business School. We discussed scenarios for currency developments several times, for instance. Sam also perhaps considered me a relatively close family member, having no children himself. My mother, Sam's cousin, also seemed to be a good friend (a "Sunday cousin").

Having inherited an ownership share in SUR, I consolidated this as follows: first, I inherited 0.5% of additional SUR shares from my mother (which were all the shares in SUR she held). Then, I purchased around 33% of the firm's shares from four senior SUR executives (they had inherited these from Sam). Finally, I purchased the remaining shares, around 26%, from various others, financed by a loan from Oslo Savings Bank, with my other shares in SUR as collateral. These shares were in "free float." So, by 1996, I owned 100% of SUR.

What was the strategy for SUR? It should be acknowledged that SUR was never considered to be a ship-owning firm of any significant size. Further, while not in imminent financial crisis, the firm's balance sheet was not strong when I took over. The firm had moved from an initial focus on oil tankers into offshore supply ships, in tandem with the boom that Norway experienced in offshore oil exploration from the late 1960s onward. There were also attempts to diversify into bulk carriers (successful) and into reefers (less successful). Over time, SUR ended up focusing exclusively on the platform supply ship (PSV) segment of offshore supply, withdrawing from the anchor handling segment. In general, this was a successful strategy.

In order to be closer to the oil offshore drilling activities in the North Sea, SUR developed a working relationship with J. Hagenaes Rederi in

Aalesund, and the firm was eventually also relocated from Oslo to Aalesund. SUR's CEOs/Presidents were:

* Thure Svensson—Olso
* Odd Settevik—Oslo
* Per Lindseth—Aalesund

Before that, Samuel Ugelstad senior and then his son Sam had been the presidents of SUR.

When Sam Ugelstad died, I received a message from him: "Do not fire any of my people." My role was initially to be a board member, while Hans G. Haga (a lawyer) was the Chairman. SUR was eventually sold in 2009, at a time when the second-hand market for supply ships turned out to be exceptionally good. Mr. Per Engeset of R.S. Platou (now Clarkson-Platou) facilitated this sale. At that time, SUR's fleet consisted of six PSVs, including the "Active Swan," a brand new PSV which was one of the world's largest, with a deck with an area of more than 1000 m^2!

The world production of offshore oil diminished somewhat from around 2015, when shale oil began to flood the market. Oil prices collapsed and the oil industry became more volatile. The growing realization that the heavy CO2 emissions from the burning of fossil fuels were a major contributor to global warming also resulted in the further marginalization of oil. Oil exploration from more marginal oil fields was dramatically scaled back. Offshore exploration in the North Sea was one of the fields that was hardest hit by this. As a result, the offshore supply ship industry was also sent into a crisis, with collapsing freight rates and a massive oversupply of ships. While this development was impossible for me to forecast when SUR was sold, it was definitely a stroke of good luck for me as SUR's owner that the firm was sold before this industry collapsed.

S. Ugelstad Invest (SUI) (2009–2021)

This is a portfolio investment company, wholly owned by me until 2021, when my son, Per Frithjof, and my daughter, Anne Sophie, each took over 49% of the ownership. Part of my motivation for making this change in ownership arose when political parties on the left took a majority in the Norwegian Parliament in the fall of 2021, with the imminent danger of a reintroduction of a potentially punitive inheritance tax. Most of my other assets were also transferred to SUI. My children received a 49% ownership share in SUI as gifts from me. Incidentally, they also were gifted my mountain apartment in Verbier, Switzerland. My relatively advanced age (78 years) was also a contributing factor to this change in ownership. I retained the position of Chairman of SUI's board, however.

SUI focuses on investing in five specific areas: stocks/bonds, real estate, shipping, ventures, and educational businesses. The bulk of the firm's investments are in the shipping and ventures categories, with a targeted rate of return, after tax, of at least 8% p.a. The main reason for this focus on the five business areas was to be able to build up a deeper level of knowledge in each area, rather than the fact that these areas also traditionally tended to provide good returns.

As noted, a generational transition was one of the reasons for the change of ownership in SUI. In order for SUI, and thereby my children, to draw ongoing benefits from whatever experience I have, I retained a 2% ownership in SUI so that I could remain as Chairman/CEO. The President/COO of the company is my son, Per Frithjof Lorange. He has more than 20 years of experience in SUI's business domain, working alongside me. It has always been a true joy to work with my son, and certainly a great source of satisfaction. We seldom have fundamental disagreements. Instead, we continuously discuss ways of "making good even better". I will return to this topic in more detail in Chap. 8. My son-in-law, Frode Lervik, is a member of SUI's strategy committee. He is also the President/CEO of Deltager, one of the firms in SUI's venture portfolio (33% ownership). My son-in-law brings logic and experience to the table; a good complement to the skills and experience of my son and myself. My daughter brings creativity. As a successful artist, she often sees things from a different angle than the rest of us, which is generally truly valuable. It gives me a great deal of satisfaction to work with my family.

SUI now operates from Sandefjord, Norway, a small city around one hour to the southwest of Oslo. It has always been SUI's philosophy to draw extensively on outside expertise when needed, rather than to add to our own staff numbers. We believe that SUI is better served this way. For instance, the transfer of ownership of SUI from me to my two children, a rather complex legal affair, was carried out by Mr. Odd Gleditsch d. y.[1] esq., a leading lawyer based in Sandefjord, who is also Chairman and the largest shareholder in Jotun A/S, the world-leading paints and coating manufacturer, also based in Sandefjord. Why did I choose Odd to assist us with this transition? Let me explain some of the reasons:

* He is an experienced lawyer (61 years old) and a senior partner in the notable law firm of Tenden, based in Tønsberg and Sandefjord. This firm possesses all the competences in-house to manage the rather complicated challenge of finding practical and simple ways to implement this generational transition.
* Odd is well versed in challenges facing families in business, being the leading member of his own family business in Jotun.
* He is a likeable person. I first met him some 20 years ago when I was a consultant to Jotun on strategic issues.

It has always been my philosophy to establish an effective working relationships with individuals who seem to have had business success. For instance, I had a close relationship with Mr. Ingvar Kamprad, the founder of IKEA. We co-owned Christiania Eiendomsselskap (a property ownership company). Together, we also held significant co-investments in the Stockholm-based pharmaceutical firm, Affibody. Further, SUI has close relationships with the Bodd Group, jointly investing with them in Deltager, as well as in their medical ventures fund, Serendipity Partners. SUI has also worked closely with Dr. Paul Eckbo, investing in several ventures where he held majority ownership (Marsoft, Preferred Global Health (PGH), Global LNG Services (GLS)). In general, SUI's strategy has increasingly evolved toward focusing on investments with relatively "predictable" risks, and with cash flows from established revenue-generating activities. As noted, this includes cooperating with individuals who are "proven" performers in their particular businesses, such as Alain Würgler (Zurich)—stocks, Morten Astrup (London)—bonds (Storm

---

[1] The title "d.y." is a Norwegian convention, to denote that a person is the third generation with the same given name, i.e., Odd; son: Odd jr.; grandson: Odd d.y.

60   P. Lorange

Bond Fund), Jan William Denstad (Lillesand)—shipping (Sole), Alex Steinberg (Boston)—US real estate (RCG), as well as Tony Andersson (Zurich)—Swiss real estate (Turnqey). SUI is generally quite conservative when it comes to investing in start-ups/early phase businesses, however.

While SUI can generally be seen as having been successful, I should briefly point out that there have been investments that represented failures, such as:

* *A vacation home project in Bulgaria.* Here the timing was wrong (they were hit by the 2008 global depression when it came to selling the apartments). The design of the apartment units was not optimal either (Scandinavian style—too spacious).
* *Sargas.* A company that had come up with a set of patents for the more effective cleaning of CO_2 emissions from power plants and various industrial installations. In this case, it turned out that a small start-up from Norway was simply not credible enough to be able to "land" projects that would require relatively large investments in very large air cleaning infrastructures. It turned out, however, that a small Sweden-based subsidiary of Sargas—Capsol—was able to take over some of Sargas' technology patents and to go public based on these. Some of SUI's losses were recuperated in the end.
* *A-Beauty and Reebate, two start-up ventures.* Here the initial valuations of the firms were perhaps too high, coupled with a lack of control of expenses and with insufficient revenues to support these, i.e., too high a "burn rate." The management and the board's lack of willingness to adjust early on might also have been a factor.

I have often reflected on whether there might be something positive to come out of failures. Failures are typically painful to face up to, but they have often given me valuable new insights. Learning from failure is key. Negative outcomes deserve careful analysis! This can be particularly difficult, given that projects that ultimately failed were generally entered into with enthusiasm, confidence, and great hope. Thus, facing up to a reality that differs from what one might have expected can be emotionally hard. But such sentiments must be overcome to avoid ending up in denial, unrealistically "explaining things away."

Other Family Business Activities

Olsen and Ugelstad, Oslo (Shipowners)

Olsen and Ugelstad was a major ship-owning company, with a fleet of more than 40 ships at its peak in the 1960s, but it went bankrupt in 1974. The company's co-founder was my grandfather, Mr. Rudolf Ugelstad. I was on the board for more than 20 years but was never an active member of the firm's management. Two of my uncles, Rolf and Trygve Ugelstad, as well as my two cousins, Rudolf and Paal, were managers. In my opinion, a mistake was made when the firm resisted evolving from a heritage business to becoming more of a firm with a portfolio of investments.

A/S Sydfjell, as well as Real Estate Properties in Ulvøysund and Salmeli

The Sydfjell firm is owned by my two sisters, Helene and Anne, and me. We inherited this business from our mother. The main assets in the firm are shares in the Olsen and Ugelstad Ship-owning Group. These are now worthless. The firm does, however, own 60% of the shares in A/S Store Stabekk Eiendom. My two sisters and I also inherited two vacation homes from our mother. Ulvøsund, a beachfront property in Lillesund in the south of Norway, is around 24 DA in size. The second property, Salmeli, is a hunting property in Kvinesdal, in Norway's southern mountainous region, and is around 5000 DA^2 in size. This property had initially been acquired by my grandfather, Rudolf Ugelstad, in 1951.

This constellation of joint real estate ownership allows my sisters and me to maintain a harmonious relationship, as we keep in close contact regarding the use and maintenance of the properties, as well as often have joint Christmas celebrations. Sydfjell was set up by my late mother and this firm has always been run in a harmonious way. I am very close to my two sisters. Hence, co-owning Sydfjell with them is a joy.

---

[2] 1 DA is the equivalent of 1000 m^2.

Store Stabekk (Hövik, Norway)

This is an approximately 100 DA large agricultural property just outside Oslo, previously owned by my grandfather, Frithjof Lorange. The way in which the inheritance of the farm was apportioned was perhaps not fair, with five of my grandfather's grandchildren getting virtually nothing, whereas the sixth inherited almost the entire farm. I had given up my rights of ownership preferences as the oldest son (as did my father), having felt that an equal split between the six cousins was perhaps the only fair way forward. In this way, all six grandchildren would be treated equally when it came to their inheritance. It has now been established, through a legal process, that the property is jointly owned by all six parties, although the one cousin that had been initially awarded most of the property now manages the farm as an agricultural property on behalf of all of us. A property development firm, A/S Store Stabekk Eiendom, has been established with the other five cousins having equal ownership. I am Chairman of this firm.

Key Learnings

I have come away with what I consider to be two overriding insights from this discussion of S. Ugelstad Rederi, S. Ugelstad Invest, and family business issues in this chapter:

* Switching from a so-called heritage business to a family-owned portfolio business seems key to the survival of the firms in which I have been involved. This allows investors, such as the members of an asset-owning family, to spread risks in order to be less dependent on one particular business. It also makes it easier to carry out ownership transition between generations, in the sense that it is easier to split a portfolio of assets into more or less equal parts, rather than having to cope with having several owners of one monolithic heritage business.

- Timing is everything. It was clearly a factor in my successful sale of S. Ugelstad Rederi. For S. Ugelstad Invest, timing considerations were particularly critical when it came to success, as well as to failure.
- Making choices to ensure that business strategies do not become too complicated is key. "Strategy means choice," as I often say. But this is, of course, typically rather hard and requires discipline.

On a more personal note, I can see how important it has been for me to be centrally involved in the S. Ugelstad businesses. The group was established more than 93 years ago. I increasingly appreciate the fact that I am a custodian, striving to pass on a firm that is in good order to the next generation. This custodianship perspective has become more and more important to me (Jaffe, 2020).

In terms of a business school curriculum, perhaps the central focus should shift toward privately held firms, family businesses, rather than majoring in public firms, which is the more usual focus. Many key business factors can more easily be discussed in the context of family businesses, including the critical importance of timing and maintaining focus when it comes to making decisions in family-owned portfolio businesses. As we shall see later, maintaining focus seems to be critical for a successful art collection too.

7

Board Membership and Consulting Assignments

To be a member of a board of directors, alternatively an advisory board, might offer invaluable learning experiences. Not only might one be privy to the firm's strategy and performance, but also be in a unique position to consider opportunities as well as threats. And there are typically other board members to learn from. Their experiences may be diverse and valuable.

Consulting offers may offer the same potential for learning as might be the case with board memberships. Outside consulting advice might be sought from various resources, with the intent to come up with a strengthened strategic focus for the firm. As a person with relatively unique knowledge, from my education, research and practice, I was fortunate enough to be offered interesting roles both as a board member as well as a consultant, now to be discussed.

Boards

In addition to serving on the boards of various family-owned corporations as a member or a chairman, I have also been a member of some significant nonfamily-related boards, some of which are publicly traded firms, including one of Europe's largest business schools.

© The Author(s), under exclusive license to Springer Nature Switzerland AG 2022
P. Lorange, *Learning and Teaching Business*,
https://doi.org/10.1007/978-3-031-14564-3_7

66   P. Lorange

Let me share with you my rationale for taking on these board positions. There were basically three reasons:

Learning: Being a board member was a great opportunity for me to learn about diverse types of businesses, particularly when it came to the strategic challenges they were facing. I was particularly interested in finding out how more effective implementation of strategies might take place, often driven by investment decisions. The insights I gained were extremely useful, particularly for my work as Chairman of S. Uglestad Invest.

Networking: There were typically several extraordinarily gifted individuals on the boards on which I served. These individuals became role models for me, and sources of inspiration. Contact with these individuals was often helpful to me in later situations, and we often developed a strong sense of camaraderie!

Prestige: I will not hide the fact that I was flattered when asked to join a board. It was always a source of gratification that others saw me as being an attractive member of their board group.

So, in sum, most of these board assignments gave me a wider network of contacts, strengthened my motivation, and appealed to my sense of self-esteem. Leaving a board was often difficult. There were often external factors beyond my control that dictated this, such as when new owners came in (ISS, Keystone), or when I was simply asked to step down (Kvaerner). However, in general, I tended to be keen to exit when I felt that the learning curve from being on a particular board was flattening out.

Kvaerner (Oslo/London)

This was an industrial conglomerate with a focus on making industrial plant machinery and equipment for the offshore industry. I served on this board for around 10 years, during which time Kvaerner took over the London-based conglomerate Trafalgar House. Kaspar Kielland was the Chairman (ex-President and CEO of A/S Elkem, an Oslo-based conglomerate that was the world's leading producer of ferroalloys). Erik Tönseth (ex-SVP and former head of the fertilizer division, Norsk Hydro) was the President and CEO. The latter had quite an unusual approach, with very little written down—most of what he did was drawn from memory! Regrettably, in the end the company ran into problems, partly due to changing market conditions, but also due to too high a leverage. Ultimately, the company was taken over by the Aker Group, another Oslo-based conglomerate.

Knud I. Larsen (Copenhagen): Diversified Shipping Company

This ship-owning firm was active in three shipping segments, all involving relatively small, specialized ships: container feeders, small LPG carriers, and small chemical tankers. All three segments were initially quite profitable but were perhaps too easy for others to enter due to the relatively low investment required for such small ships. When the freight markets in all three segments collapsed, almost simultaneously, and costs were also too high, the firm went bankrupt. This was a shock! To have a relatively low break-even level for one's business became a key learning for me.

Royal Caribbean Cruise Lines (RCCL) (Miami)

RCCL is the world's second-largest owner and operator of cruise ships after Carnival Cruises. For a while, it was owned primarily by three groups: Anders Wilhelmsen (shipowners, Oslo), the Pritzker Group (Hyatt Hotels and much more, Chicago), and the Ofer Group (shipowners, London). I was nominated to serve on this board by Anders Wilhelmsen, a position I held for around six years. The combination of superb marketing, excellence in operations, and continuous product innovations yielded strong results for RCCL, and also taught me a lot.

Seaspan (Vancouver/Hong Kong)

Seaspan is the world's largest owner of large container ships, has a fleet of more than 80 modern container ships, chartered out to leading container line operators. The company's business was quite analogous to aircraft leasing. The Chairman when I was serving on the board was Mr. Kyle Washington, representing the dominant owners, the Washington Group (Vancouver). The President and CEO was Gerry Wang, originally from Shanghai. I served on this board for around ten years. More and more of the company's business came to be focused on China—building ships there, financing them with Chinese banks, chartering them to Chinese container line operators (COSCO, China Shipping, later merged into one company, named COSCO). Most of Seaspan's operations were moved to Hong Kong in 2010.

ISS (Copenhagen)

This was the world's largest company operating in the cleaning business, focusing primarily on hospitals, schools, hotels, and so on, as well as on industrial cleaning. There were also related businesses in flood damage control, landscaping, pesticide control, and cleaning of water/sewage pipes. The company had a particularly strong position in Europe. A combined hostile takeover by EQT Partners and Goldman Sacks led to my resignation from the Board in 2015 after some six years.

I had little or no direct ownership stake in any of these companies. The way for me was to consider myself to "represent" the ownership side, a key role for board members, to always try to act like someone who could contribute to better decisions being made, and to support the CEO, so that they might be able to move forward more successfully. I often felt a sense of pressure while serving on these boards, however, in that I seemed to be expected to come up with new insights that I simply did not have! So, I was often relatively silent. At times, this led to personal anxiety—was I too passive?

I was also a board member for a range of other organizations:

Citicorp Norway/International (Oslo, London)

I was Chairman at Citicorp Norway from 1989 to 1992, and then a member of the Board of Citibank International (London) from 1998 to

7 Board Membership and Consulting Assignments 69

2000. When I became a member of this Board's credits subcommittee, I experiences that the workload became too great and I decided to resign. A key learning point here is that being a good board member often requires a lot of work, putting in the necessary hours, for example, in the preparation of board documents. At times, this workload was not realistically achievable, given the many other tasks that I had. The Board's overriding focus was quite similar to that found in most large banks, namely avoiding major mistakes. This rather extreme risk-averse corporate culture meant that my motivation came to be relatively low in the end.

Copenhagen Business School

Copenhagen Business School (CBS) is Europe's largest independent business school, owned by the Danish government. The Rector (President) during my time on the board was Dr. Finn Junge-Jensen. While successful and dynamic as an academic institution, the school's faculty were perhaps rather conventional, even a little conservative. The Board spent a lot of time focusing on an ultimately failed merger proposal for CBS to join Copenhagen University. This was proposed and "promoted" by Denmark's Ministry of Education. I served on this Board for around 10 years and was also awarded an honorary doctorate from CBS. I stepped down in 2015. A key learning for me: How actions from politicians and members of the public sector can have a significant impact.

Co Co Co (Copenhagen)

This management consulting firm was chaired by General Kristian Widt, former head of Denmark's armed forces. I served on this company's board for four years, and left when the firm merged with a competitor, to take on a new name, Granit. This was in 2016. A key learning for me was the fact that mergers, as well as being acquired, tend to be rather unpredictable to foresee!

I ended up being on several Danish boards (Knud I. Larsen A/S, ISS A/S, Copenhagen Business School, Co Co Co). Why was this? Perhaps I had gained a certain positive reputation in Denmark over the years, but the language was a particular challenge. While the Scandinavian languages are quite similar, the intonations are typically rather different. So, it is simply not that easy for Danes and Norwegians to understand each other. This meant that I had to concentrate a great deal when listening to the debates at the board meetings. I often spoke in English when I gave my inputs, and this was well understood by all. Board meetings involved, nevertheless, feats of concentration for me, and I often came away with a headache!

I was also on the board and/or had ownership positions in the following three companies:

IKO Strategi (Oslo)

I was Chairman of this major Norwegian management consulting firm for five years. Mr. Per Hatling was President and then moved on to become President and CEO of Tine, Norway's largest dairy company. I ended my Chairmanship when Mr. Hatling left.

Globalpraxis (Barcelona)

This management consulting firm was run by Jean-Paul Evrard (from Liege, Belgium) and Ramon Vergés (from Girona, Spain). I had a small ownership position (15%) and was also on the firm's board. Globalpraxis was the world leader when it came to improving routes to market. Clients were generally leading consumer products companies. The firm was highly successful for many years but was hit hard by the COVID-19 pandemic, largely because of the severe travel restrictions that were imposed across most of the world then. To sell my share in early 2021 was not an easy decision for me. I had worked with one of the two founder-owners, Ramon Vergés, for a long time, stemming back to work we did together at San Miguel many years earlier. I had become good friends with both of the other founder-owners. It was an important lesson for me that mixing friendship and ownership can be hard. In this instance, fortunately, we separated on good terms.

Keystone (Oslo)

Keystone is an Oslo-based software company which owns a search engine that matches students with academic institutions to better align particular students' interests with actual academic offerings. The business has a worldwide scope. The company also offers services to specific academic institutions to support their student recruiting processes. The President and CEO, up until 2020, was Linus Murphy and the Chairman was Torstein Berg. The venture firm Viking took a significant position in 2020, bringing in its own Chairman and putting in a new President, Erik Harrell. The result was more aggressive growth. I served on this board from 2015 to 2020. SUI is now the owner of a relatively small share in the company. For me, a key learning was the importance of bringing in new managers/owners, and capital that might stimulate accelerated growth.

While the former CEO had done a good job and the firm had grown organically, it seemed to come to a point where acceleration of growth was required, perhaps to eventually "dress up" the firm for an IPO or sale. Hence, a new leader was brought in, additional capital was secured, and acquisitions were made. The Board's composition also changed and I was out! Keystone was a particularly interesting case for me, in the sense that the firm's business could be seen as very close to what we did at BI, IMD, or Lorange Institute, with all institutions being clients of Keystone at various times.

Consulting

Let us now shift focus from my work as a director on various boards, to my consulting roles. Not surprisingly, I have been involved in a relatively large number of consulting assignments, eight of which will be reported on in the following pages. These eight assignments are those which I consider I have personally benefited from the most in terms of acquiring new insights. It is all a matter of "giving more than you take." I have been privileged to be allowed to take this approach in all the consulting and/or

P. Lorange

board assignments in which I have been involved. Establishing good ongoing personal and professional relationships is key here, leading to mutual trust! Dewar, Keller, and Malhotra express the common challenge of effective work on boards as well as progressive consulting so well: "Help [...] the business" with a strong focus on the future being particularly key (2022).

Most of these consulting activities took place when I was active at one of the US-based academic institutions reported in Chap. 2. It was common practice in all these institutions for faculty members to be allowed to undertake one day of consulting per week, as long as there was no conflict of interest with the academic institution itself, of course. I was later particularly careful to avoid such potential conflicts when I was President of Norwegian School of Business (BI), and later at IMD. I would not allow myself to get into a position to compete with the institution I led!

Ericsson Radio (Stockholm)

This is a division of LM Ericsson and is the world leader in base-station networks for mobile telephony. During the period I consulted for them (1975–1980), they also had a significant presence in the so-called "intelligent" mobile phone handset business (a later joint venture with Sony which was then subsequently sold to Microsoft). My assignment was primarily that of coaching the top tier of managers in this division to implement the strategy in a more effective way by focusing on speed and stronger coordination between functions, such as marketing, sales, finance, and the division's product development efforts. The SVP in charge of the division was the legendary Dr. Åke Lundqvist, who possessed a unique combination of superb technological knowledge as well as outstanding marketing and sales capabilities and an incredible ability to inspire people within his organization. He had a PhD in radio engineering from the Royal Swedish Academy of Science and had previously attended IMEDE's annual program. For me, a key insight of learning was to better understand the importance of effective leadership, from the top.

San Miguel (Manila)

This was the largest corporate grouping in the Philippines, with the bulk of the group producing brewery products (San Miguel and other brands), with breweries located in the Philippines, Hong Kong, and Spain. Another part, Anscor, was primarily involved in the mining/extraction business (copper, gold, etc.). The CEO was initially Andrés Soriano Jr. ("Mr. Andy") and, subsequently, his son, Andrés Soriano d.y. ("Andy"). I worked with the group from 1991 to 1996, primarily supporting their efforts to implement a more effective strategic planning process, based on a strong strategic focus within each of the group's businesses. Mr. Andy and his son Andy were both Wharton graduates. This probably had a lot to do with my selection for this assignment. But the geographic distance between Manila and Philadelphia was significant and made the assignment a stressful one for me as well as for others.

This was the first time that I had worked with both the owner and his son. Mr. Andy, unfortunately, had brain cancer and passed away in the middle of the project. I also worked closely with Mr. Andy's other two sons, Eduardo and Carlos, as well as with the top professional management teams of the two groups run by the Sorianos. A key learning for me was finding strategic solutions that all key stakeholders could live with. The unstable political situation in the Philippines also gave rise to doubts about what the future might hold. For instance, at one point, San Miguel was "confiscated" by another group of owners who were more friendly to the government that was then in power. All in all, I learned a lot about how limitations deriving from key stakeholders—owners, managers, and governments—might impact on decisions about which strategic paths to follow.

Elkem (Oslo)

This industrial corporation was the world's leading producer of ferroalloys and was also a relatively large producer of aluminum. In addition, the company was involved in a wide array of other businesses, all relatively small (mining, manufacturing of locks and trailers, insulation materials, among other things). Most of the firm's wide array of business activities were the result of mergers and/or joint ventures over the years (merger with Christiania Spigerverk, joint venture with Alcoa and Rockwood, purchase of Union Carbide's ferroalloy activities, etc.). My job was to assist the firm's leadership in developing a more robust business portfolio and to help the various businesses to come up with more effective business strategies, ideally based on a common strategic planning approach. This assignment lasted some five years and was judged by many to be successful. The importance of focusing on a clear, well-defined strategy ("strategy means choice") became a key insight.

Reflecting further on this assignment, which took place some time ago now, I am struck by the relevance of what the American academic and writer Abigail McCarthy said, "every memoir reminds us of faraway and long ago, of loss and change, of persons and places beyond recall" (McCarthy, 1971). I was, of course, relatively inexperienced when I became involved with Elkem. The approach that I took was inspired by my doctoral research at Harvard. I had refined this thinking further in the course of some earlier consulting work, primarily done for the Newsweek Publishing Group. Two additional key learnings stand out for me:

* It was essential to have the total support of the CEO, in this case, Elkem's Mr. Kaspar Kielland. Having the opportunity to work with him, and particularly to benefit from the many excellent discussions we had, was of great value to me. Kaspar was later instrumental in getting me onto the boards of Kvaerner as well as Royal Caribbean, as well in as recommending me to Borregaard.
* Despite his outstanding qualities, Kaspar once called several of the smaller strategic entities in Elkem's business portfolio "peripheral businesses." It was revelatory for me to observe the negative motivational effect this had on the businesses involved. Never single out businesses in this way or indicate that they might be up for sale (until it actually takes place). This has become an important guideline for me. See Chap. 6, in particular, for how this was handled when S. Ugelstad Rederi was sold.

7 Board Membership and Consulting Assignments

Borregaard (Sarpsborg)

My consulting assignment with Borregaard was, in many ways, similar to my involvement at Elkem, namely, to assist the firm in coming up with more focused strategies, designed around a common strategic planning system for all divisions (pulp, forest-based products, paper, pheromones, mining, and chemicals). Mr. Rein Sørhus was the President and CEO and he gave me his full support. This process was, however, "disrupted" when the firm was unexpectedly taken over by Orkla in 1986. My involvement thus lasted for one year only. It should be noted that Borregaard had a long standing in Norway's business world and was one of the country's largest firms. Might a clearer strategy on Borregaard's behalf have better signaled the firm's true value? Perhaps my own involvement might have played a role here in that I should perhaps have been firmer. A key learning, indeed, was that takeovers and mergers, often taking place quite unexpectedly, might slow down and disrupt such strategic focusing.

Norsk Hydro (Oslo)

Norsk Hydro, Norway's largest industrial group, was involved in the manufacturing of fertilizers, light metals (aluminum and magnesium), and was also active in offshore oil exploration. The company had taken over A/S Årdal og Sunndal Verk, a large aluminum smelter, as well as Norway's third largest offshore oil exploration company, Saga Petroleum. The Norwegian government owned a majority of the firm's shares. They subsequently decided that the firm's oil-related business should be taken over by Statoil (now Equinor), also government controlled. Subsequently, the fertilizer activities were spun off to become Yara A/S. The aluminum activities were further consolidated through the purchase of Orkla's downstream aluminum business. The "new" Hydro was thus a large integrated aluminum manufacturer. My assignment was to assist the top management group of five when it came to the future development of the group's strategies, in essence acting as a catalyst/outside member within this corporate team. In particular, I was a consultant to Mr. Egil

76   P. Lorange

Myklebust, the firm's President and CEO, but also to the entire top management team. It should be mentioned that I also served as a member of the company's board of representatives from 1989 until 2005, when this institutional "layer" was phased out. For me to gain more detailed insights regarding evolutionary strategic efforts from the top of managerial "pyramid" was an invaluable experience.

Michelin (Clermont-Ferrand, France)

This French company, headquartered in Clermont-Ferrand, is one is the world's largest tire manufacturers and is also the publisher of the famous *Guide Michelin*. My assignment was to provide its top leadership with input regarding how to organize the company's US operations. It was interesting for me to observe that this successful firm was managed by a team of three, one of whom was always drawn from the Michelin family, with this small committee acting as the firm's CEO. There was approximately ten years difference between these three individuals. Thus, experience, drive, and long-term thinking were covered. My main contact was François Michelin, who was in the middle of the age range in the three-person CEO team at the time.

I gained invaluable experience from this assignment also. In particular, I observed how family and nonfamily members were able to work together constructively for the first time. The "CEO by committee of three" approach was an eye-opener, allowing for a combination of stakeholder interests when it came to family concerns, business acumen, and experience! Particularly, how did they approach the refocusing of Michelin's strategy relating to the core US market?

Tine (and previously Øglaend, Sandnes) (Oslo)

These two assignments both involved complete strategic shifts and my key contact was the firm's CEO, Mr. Per Hatling. For me, a key learning was the importance of "selling in" such major strategic shifts to the others in those firms' organizations.

Pechiney (Paris)

Pechiney was a large Paris-based manufacturer of steel, titanium, chemicals, and an aluminum producer making high-precision components for aircraft wings and jet engine rotor blades (Howmet). My job was to support their development of a more effective strategic planning process. A focus on precision and a clear scientific analysis were an important part of this company's culture, quite typical of the very best in French corporations. For me, it was particularly interesting to see and to appreciate the "elitism" that resulted from virtually all the firm's senior executives having been educated at an Ecole Polytechnique. Everyone worked hard and pulled together, applying common values and sharp minds. I discovered that elitism could indeed be a good thing! Perhaps this is something that is fairly exclusive to France!

As noted, these and other consulting assignments largely predated my appointment as President of BI and, subsequently, IMD. There had been no sense of conflict of interest between these institutions' value-creating activities and my own private concerns. As the President of these schools, I issued clear guidelines to the faculty and staff so that they might avoid being in positions that "competed" with the institution by which they were employed, and I therefore also significantly reduced my own involvement in consultancy roles. Being in charge of a business school typically also involves bringing in new revenue-generating activities from corporate clients. Giving "free" initial advice, which might later lead to the purchasing of programs and enrollments, was therefore seen as important for me.

Key Learnings

I have already touched upon several key learning insights that I have gotten from these board roles as well as from the various consulting assignments. Much more could be said about the key learning points I extracted from the board memberships and consulting assignments discussed in this chapter. However, let me limit myself to highlight two key conclusions that stand out for me:

* In my experience, there is *not* all that much that outside board members can realistically contribute. Although this may not have become all that apparent from my earlier comments about the various boards on which I served, my experience suggests that supporting the CEO is perhaps the most critical contribution that an outside board member can make. The life of a CEO is typically quite lonely, and a board member's experience can come in handy in supporting a CEO's long-term agenda, helping them to withstand the often intensive short-term pressure to focus on the bottom line. So, I saw my role as one of supporting management and, above all, the CEO. I did try to put myself in their shoes. How could I help them to do a better job and help to bolster their self-confidence? A seminal book on this topic, CEO Excellence by three senior management consultants from McKinsey also underscore this (Dewar et al., 2022).
* Effective strategies do matter. To achieve this, I see no alternatives other than to implement effective strategic planning processes. Many have come to question strategic planning, often seeing it as overly bureaucratic (Mintzberg, 1994). I do not share this view. Strategic thinking *can* indeed be developed and carefully designed strategic processes *can* make a difference! But a clear strategic culture is perhaps more important than the use of some of the well-known strategic tools, such as so-called SWAT (strengths, weaknesses, advantages, threats) analysis, market share dominance, Porter's five forces, etc. The factors we will discuss in parts three and four of this book add up to a good example of an effective strategic culture.

So why strategy? My feeling is that it is key for most organizations to have a good sense of direction. And this means avoiding going down blind alleys. As noted, "strategy means choice." A clear strategy provides a common sense of direction for the members of an organization so that they all pull in the same direction. This approach was commented on by

7 Board Membership and Consulting Assignments

several of the lawyers in the law firm Tenden, who felt that SUI's direction, with its five focal areas of engagement, led to exceptional clarity and this was applauded by them.

What are the implications of the experiences I describe in this chapter, not only for running businesses more effectively but also for better business education? Primarily, I believe that effective business management, well-running business schools, and a focus on effective curriculum should support learning as they strive to become more proficient in strengthening firms' existing strategies, i.e., to support the strategies that are being pursued, rather than coming up with new theories that might be "disruptive."

Part III

Guiding Principles

My professional journey has led me to focus on a set of factors that I consider to be particularly important when it comes to shaping successful business strategies as well as pointing towards effective ways for running business schools and curriculum design. Why these factors in particular? My sense is that these aspects above all make for a more realistic vision. Why not include more factors? Maintaining a degree of simplicity is, of course, key. All that I can say about this is that it is a purely matter of my deductive efforts that these particular factors have been included.

Hoffman and Yeh take a somewhat narrower approach to the factors which might have implications for strategic success. In their book *Blitzscaling* (2018), they propose that rapid growth is key, and that being the first in the field to do so is critical to achieving strategic success. While I agree that speed and innovation are factors in this process, I take a relatively broader view and have identified other factors in my guiding principles. Wernerfelt also sees the value of strategic resources when analyzing a firm's likelihood of success, as stated in his seminal paper *A Resource-based View of the Firm* (1984). Hamel and Prahalad (2005) argue that Western companies focus on trimming their ambitions to match resources and, as a result, search only for advantages they can sustain.

82   Guiding Principles

In my opinion, the nine critical success factors that we will discuss in Parts Three and Four, perhaps seen as a manifestation of a company's culture, are typically more important than traditional strategic factors (such as Porter's five factors, SWOT analysis, focus on dominant market share, and so on). Business success seems much more fundamentally to be a function of a healthy corporate culture. Each of the critical success factors seems to be essential in determining such business success, however.

Is there a body of research which might corroborate this? While I am not aware of any research-based conclusions, there seems to be strong experiential "evidence" to confirm this (see Freedman, 2013, in particular). Key learning points throughout my career, as discussed in Parts One and Two, have also led me to this conclusion. My own experiences as a business leader, as well as consulting and board experiences, further seem to point in this direction.

What about any interrelationships between the critical success factors? While we will discuss these in turn, they largely seem to be interrelated, rather than to be seen as separate. They are not independent silos (Aaker, 2008; Tett, 2015). A winning corporate culture encompasses all factors.

This brings me to an important related issue. It seems that when we focus on only one, or a few, of these factors, the culture as a whole may still be strengthened. The other factors may also be positively impacted! This represents an important insight when it comes to good management practice, namely that coping with one particular critical success factor might lead to a much broader "solution" being achieved. So, the key is to thoroughly strengthen particular individual factors so that a much broader strengthening of the entire culture might be achieved. This relates not only to inputs for good practices for running businesses as well as business schools, but also for modern curricular design for business schools. More *fundamentally*, this involves the identification of a set of factors that future generations can focus on to be successful. Thus, Parts Three and Four provide what in essence might be considered a list of key attributes for aspiring successful executives.

While there might be a relatively high degree of agreement regarding the above, several prominent experts on strategy seem to take a somewhat narrower view. For instance, Rumelt (2011) suggests detecting one or two "pivot points" to focus on, and to then concentrate action and resources on them, is the key to good strategy. While this may be considered to be a good "rule of thumb", I have found relative success in my broader approach, as detailed in the following chapter.

8

Quality of Education, Career, Business, and Art

Striving for quality has always been an important guiding principle for me. I feel that this has been reflected in many different ways throughout my life, first as a younger man, when it came to my choice of educational institutions and my job choices and later, regarding how business was conducted, and so on. This ambition has also guided me when it comes to my art collection, and even when it came to choosing where to live. One might even say that this guided who I ended up with as partners in life, too! This argument should obviously not be taken too far, however.

Let us look at all of this in more detail.

Educational Choices

When I was around 20 years old, I had to choose which institutions to apply to for my undergraduate education. Being Norwegian and having grown up in this country, I had been somewhat "indoctrinated" with the dictum that Norway's educational offerings were among the world's best. In retrospect, I have come to realize that this is not necessarily the case. But at the time a strong domestic bias guided my decision-making! For

© The Author(s), under exclusive license to Springer Nature Switzerland AG 2022
P. Lorange, *Learning and Teaching Business*,
https://doi.org/10.1007/978-3-031-14564-3_8

instance, the "best" place to study medicine would be the University of Oslo, engineering should be studied at the Norwegian Technical University in Trondheim, and business at the Norwegian School of Economics and Business Administration (NHH) in Bergen, and so on. Since I had a particular interest in studying business, I applied to NHH and was accepted, as one of 129 new undergraduates (today the annual intake exceeds 400 students!). I completed my studies in three years, still believing that NHH represented the best there was. This view was, indeed, reinforced throughout my entire period of study there.

Later, I applied to Yale and was accepted onto this university's Operations Analysis program (at that time, within the Department of Administration Science, which later became Yale's Business School). I had also applied to MIT's Sloan School of Management as well as to Harvard Business School (HBS) but was turned down by both places. Unbeknown to me, my father and uncles played significant roles in supporting my applications by writing letters of support to back up my applications. Apparently, my uncles emphasized that they saw me as an open-minded, agile fellow, eager to learn, above all about business.

I arrived full of optimism on Yale's campus in New Haven in the fall of 1967. However, I soon came to realize that going for a PhD in such a specialized, mathematics-driven field as that offered in Operations Analysis did not sufficiently coincide with my real interest—business! So, I settled for a master's degree instead, which was obtained after one year of study, and then applied to Harvard Business School's doctoral program. This time I was accepted! Having a degree from Yale must have had a more positive impact on the admissions officer than the initial degree from NHH! I completed my doctoral studies at HBS in three years, but only after much hard work! This was, however, my next important career step.

Significantly, I came to realize that much of what I had learnt at NHH did not, in general, seem to be at the cutting edge. So, I had to "relearn" quite a lot of material. This was an eye-opener for me. I came to understand that the United States as an internationally networked nation—and, in fact, a much larger and richer one than Norway—would have many more leading high-quality academic institutions than smaller, relatively peripheral places such as Norway! This realization has influenced

8 Quality of Education, Career, Business, and Art

my outlook ever since, namely, to try to be part of "where it happens" internationally. *Diversity* seems to be a key driver here. And diversity is more readily achievable in large, wealthy, open-societal settings such as the United States, the United Kingdom, or even where I now live, in Switzerland, with its small "sub"-nationalities (German, French, Italian, Romansch). As Bjørnsson says "everything that we look at takes on different shapes depending on where one[self] is located... To learn means to be inspired by what others' eyes are seeing. This means that learning in this open-minded way is key. If not, we would be the losers!" (Bjørnsson, 1892).

Jobs

My first academic job was at IMEDE, a leading international business school located in Lausanne, Switzerland. I had earlier already had a full-time job as a research assistant at NHH from 1966–1967, in the school's Economic Geography department. However, in my own thinking this job basically represented a year of preparing myself for studies in the United States. IMEDE was a great experience, with a strong international team of leading academic colleagues and international executive students drawn from leading firms worldwide. Getting such varied exposure to cutting-edge managerial challenges was great for me!

However, as previously mentioned, I was let go from IMEDE after only two years. In the end, it all worked out for the best, as I was then forced to apply for new positions and ended up as an assistant professor (later associate professor) at the Sloan School of Management, MIT. Carrying out cutting-edge research was the sine qua non at Sloan. And this research was designed to be inspired by *and* to inspire the school's other faculty members, i.e., *not* done in splendid isolation! To be part of such a stimulating and generally quite cross-disciplinary setting was indeed an eye-opener for me. However, my own research efforts were probably insufficient and were carried out in isolation rather than collaboratively. Hence, it was perhaps no surprise that I was later denied tenure. However, I then moved to the Wharton School, University of Pennsylvania, initially as an associate professor *with* tenure and subsequently as a full professor, eventually holding an endowed professorial chair, the William Wurster Professor of International Business. I also became head of the Lauder Institute, a joint undertaking between the Wharton School and the University of Pennsylvania's School of Arts and Sciences. This has all been discussed in detail in Chap. 2.

At Wharton, I was able to work with truly talented students from all over the world, another great experience for me. In my time there, I came to appreciate that hard work and academic excellence typically go hand in hand. My appetite to try to enhance quality through leadership was also developed while at Wharton. I was appointed Chairman of the school's largest academic department, the Management Department, with Strategy, Organizational Behavior, Technology Management, Labor Relations, and Entrepreneurship as its five multi-foci. Here, the task was very similar to that of a coach for a leading soccer team—finding strong new faculty members, letting non-performers go, working with each remaining individual on their research and teaching, giving feedback, encouraging them, and so on. I also became head of Wharton's International Center, where the focus was on doing cutting-edge research on international managerial problems as well as developing links with leading schools worldwide to better pursue this. Helping to catalyze Wharton's own faculty to orient themselves more internationally was perhaps the most stimulating aspect of this job. The International Center subsequently became the William Wurster Center and, as noted, I became the holder of the William Wurster endowed professorial chair.

It was natural for me to try to build further on this experience to find ways of improving the quality of various aspects of other academic institutions. By now, I had the ambition to try to run a full-fledged business school myself. So, I agreed to stand for election as President of BI in Oslo. I was indeed elected to the position, but only by a narrow margin. As previously discussed, a move back to Norway was also a motivating factor.

It turned out that many of the challenges I had encountered at Wharton were similar to those that I now faced at BI, particularly when it came to being an "effective coach," perhaps especially grappling with prima donna tendencies among some faculty members ("silos"). But there was one additional issue that I had never grappled with before, namely, trying to maintain high standards while keeping costs low! This issue, by the way,

8 Quality of Education, Career, Business, and Art

has remained key for me ever since! BI's network of regional satellite campuses located in 11 different sites in Norway, with its main campus in Oslo as the "hub in the wheel," represented one "solution." New programs were developed at the "hub" by BI's experienced academic staff there. These generally incorporated rather traditional but nevertheless high-quality research and pedagogical elements. Leading local business executives were then trained at the "hub" center before then being asked to deliver the programs locally. These business executives were encouraged to draw on the centrally located expert staff as needed, of course.

Further, a network-based library system was developed, with a relatively large collection of books and periodicals held in a central location. This was made available to each of the satellite campuses via the Internet so that most publications would be available more or less instantly wherever they were needed. Many administrative roles were also shared between the campuses, and the training of administrators was also system-wide. Although this network approach was certainly not perfect, it nevertheless offered a practical approach to achieving quality at a more reasonable cost. And it should be kept in mind that in 1990 this was seen as quite forward thinking.

After BI, I was asked to join IMD as its President. My experiences as President of IMD have been documented in Chap. 2. IMD, one of the world's leading business schools, had (and still has) an excellent reputation. Although it had a strong faculty as well as first-class students from all over the world, the school was and is still relatively small. For me, this assignment (which lasted for 15 years) represented another clear opportunity to "go for quality." The main improvements required at IMD were to build on quality by recruiting even better faculty, to introduce even stronger programs, even more innovative teaching materials, even better administrative routines, and so on. The cost side was not so much of a priority during my tenure as president, beyond running an effective operation. By the end of my first years as IMD's president, there seemed to be a broad consensus that I had been relatively successful. Eventually, I was appointed Honorary President, the only person to be awarded this honor in IMD's history (November 2021).

It would be helpful to look in more detail at the dilemma of achieving both high quality *and* low cost. After the end of my stint at IMD, I became involved in two large-scale "experiments" that both explored new ways of developing the "business school of the future." This effort was, of course, in part motivated by observing the rapidly rising tuition fees at most business schools. How might such increasing costs be contained by integrating effective new technologies into the operation of business schools? And how might one incorporate new cutting-edge pedagogical advances in a speedy and efficient way? Changes in students' learning preferences, particularly when it came to learning on the job rather than taking time off from work also stimulated my thought processes as I searched for new ways to deliver on business education and the modern curriculum!

The first experiment, Lorange Institute, involved taking over a business school with an existing campus in Horgen, on the shore of Lake Zurich. There were no permanent full-time professors at Lorange Institute, but rather a network of capable academicians drawn from other leading business schools, as well as from practice. These individuals were then engaged to deliver in their areas of expertise on an "as needed" basis. Thus, significant costs were avoided by not having faculty "sitting around perhaps in idle ways for longer periods of time." The curriculum was modularized and courses were offered in a condensed form, so that participants were generally able to learn while remaining in their full-time jobs. Finally, the physical layout of the classrooms featured round tables on level surfaces rather than banked rows of seats to stimulate group discussion, i.e., learning based on "give and take," rather than on more passive internalization of what each professor might deliver via conventional lectures delivered in the traditional horseshoe-shaped auditorium.

The Lorange Institute was only partially successful, however. While it succeeded in delivering good quality learning to students at a reasonable cost, the Institute was unable to secure the necessary ratings to qualify as a quality offering by leading academic rating institutions, such as EFMD and AACSB. Lorange Institute's courses were rated by AMBA, however, the third-position rating institution worldwide. My sense is that the Lorange Institute's way of doing things might simply have been too radical. A major bone of contention seemed to be that the Institute would not be undertaking sufficient original research by a permanent faculty. Rather, the school would have to rely on what various faculty members were developing at their parent academic institutions. While there might be an element of truth in this, it should also be said that unique "pieces" of knowledge increasingly seem to be seen as belonging to the individual faculty members who have developed them, i.e., *not* by each academic institution, as seems to have been the case in the past.

In the end, however, the Lorange Institute was sold to CEIBS, a Shanghai-based business school, perhaps the leading school in China. CEIBS has subsequently followed a different approach to learning from the one we pioneered at Lorange Institute by closely integrating its offerings at their Horgen campus with those offered in Shanghai.

My next experiment with a low-cost/high-quality concept for a learning institution of the future was the Lorange Network (LN), which was started in 2016. As previously noted, LN was primarily focused on providing relevant content to family-owned firms, including entrepreneurial start-ups, as well as to independent investors, with a heavy focus on web-based technology. Expert panels exposed LN members to various cutting-edge issues through short online sessions. As of early 2021, there were more than 3,300 members in the network.

The LN approach seems to have been quite successful and could certainly be a prototype for a business school of the future. My decision to let IMD take over LN in mid-2021 was driven by a realization that at my age (78) its long-term viability dictated that it would be prudent to find a reputable new owner. IMD seemed ideal! The quality of future content delivered to learners would be ensured and further enhanced in this way.

Business

An emphasis on quality has, of course, been a key pillar of my business activities, initially focusing on S. Ugelstad Rederi (SUR), and subsequently S. Ugelstad Invest (SUI), both firms having been wholly owned by me.

Let us start with SUR. It was key here to always choose the best quality solutions when it came to how ships were built, equipped, and maintained. Maintenance always entailed buying original spare parts, even though these could be considerably more expensive than copies, typically manufactured in the Far East. All our ships were classified in the Norwegian Register (DnVGL), again, a mark of quality. This classification agency specified, for instance, that several steel plates in the bottom of one of SUR's ships, M/S Normandic, needed to be replaced, which was then promptly done. The British classification agency, Lloyds, which had classified the ship before SUR bought it second-hand, felt that such replacements were not necessary!

When it came to specifications for newbuilds, nothing of essence was spared, although SUR never "gold plated" its new ships by specifying features that were not necessary, even if perhaps "good to have." Engines, tank systems, and navigational equipment were always of the best quality.

SUR exclusively chartered out its ships to first-class corporations, such as ConocoPhillips, BP, or Total. And these leading firms also "approved" the ships owned by SUR as being on their list of ships that they considered to be in a good condition and of a relatively young age. Lists of "approved" ships really did exist!

One more quality-related feature should be mentioned, namely the choice of a shipbroker to support SUR, enabling me to have a reliable discussion partner when it came to important strategic decisions, such as the chartering or ordering of new ships, the sale of old ones, as well as the purchase of secondhand ships. R.S. Platou (later Clarkson-Platou), the well-known Oslo-based shipbroker, was chosen for this, with senior shipbroker Per Engeset being my key contact. Relying on top-quality advisors and business partners was an approach that was consistently followed when it came to SUR's business activities.

Let us now turn to S. Ugelstad Invest, SUI. First, it should be said that SUI always worked closely with top-rated Swiss banks, most notably Zurcher Kantonalbank, Bank Vontobel, and UBS. And SUI relied on top-performing stockbrokers, most notably Alain Würgler in Zurich, the Jockey Fund in Hong Kong, and Rune Oseid in Oslo. SUI's shipping investments were made through four key entities: Sole Shipping (Lillesand), Pareto, Clarkson-Platou (both Oslo), and Rye-Florenz (London). Our real estate activities were managed by Alex Steinberg in Boston, who runs RCG, as well as by Tony Andersson in Zurich, who runs Turnqey. In addition, SUI relied on top-quality fund managers, such as Antler in Singapore, Jockey Fund in Hong Kong, Blue Ivy Fund

8 Quality of Education, Career, Business, and Art

in Boston, and Storm Bond Fund in London. It might be deduced from the above that SUI's business model involved investing in various firms with their own operations rather than setting up its own organization to manage its investments.

Art

I have a reasonable collection of paintings and sculptures, mostly by Norwegian and other Scandinavian artists, as well as a few German and Swiss pieces. The objects that I collect are typically exhibited in one of my five residences, Küssnacht am Rigi, Pully, Verbier, Asker, or Ulvösund. Virtually nothing is stored in depots or warehouses. This makes my collection relatively small, but highly personal. Since it is all on display on the walls of my residences, the collection reflects my personal taste. Striving for quality aligned with my personal taste has been a key "leitbild" here. Most of the paintings might be classified as modern (Jorn, Bergmann, Weidemann, Förg, Rian, Richard), but there are also some more classical ones (Munch, Thaulow, Hertewig, Kröyer). I also own a few sculptures (Penk, Haukeland, Rygh). So, there is a deliberately eclectic mix. Art comes in various forms, but it generally inspires me and helps me to "see" things from different angles. Quality and eclecticism are key factors in achieving such benefits.

As I have already said, it seems important to consider things from different perspectives. Over the years, I have come to realize that there are relatively few absolute truths, whether in science, social science, business, or other areas. This seems to be the case when it comes to art too. While one artist may provoke relatively straightforward interpretations of various phenomena for the viewer, other artists may lead us in other directions. Eclecticism is again important. For this reason, I always seem to prefer art exhibitions where more than one artist's work is displayed. The works of art I enjoy typically represent more than one facet. For instance, we may not only *see* certain things (visual, physical) but also experience a psychological side ("this is mine," this represents my emotions). And there is a rational side to it as well (the "we," and how we are part of a bigger situation). This might indeed be the essence of the eclecticism of experiencing art. A key assertion for me has always been, therefore, that my art has tended to inspire me, indeed, "giving" me support when it came to various key decisions that I had to take in business as well as in academic management (Lorange, 2022a, b).

How do I source good art? And how do I ensure diversity? I have benefited greatly from the support of two leading Scandinavian auctioneers, the owner of Blomqvist in Oslo, Elisabeth Vik Forsberg, as well as the owner of Bruun-Rasmussen in Copenhagen, Jesper Bruun-Rasmussen. The Oslo-based Emilie Magnus, owner of OSL Contemporary Gallery, has also supported me a lot. Once again, working with outstanding experts often seems to pay off, and this ensures quality.

Residences

For me, the choice of comfortable homes is critical. I have two overriding criteria:

* Location, location, location.
* A minimum of maintenance, no garden for instance, and little noise. Penthouse apartments are usually preferred.

My primary residence is in Pully, where I own a penthouse that occupies the entire top floor of a building, with perfect views over Lake Geneva. Further, I have two apartments for outdoor sports, walking, and skiing, one in Verbier, Switzerland, and one at Kvitfjell, Norway, adjacent to the Olympic downhill slope. Ownership of these two apartments has recently been transferred to my two children, but I have retained preferential usage rights. Additionally, I own a penthouse apartment in Asker, Norway and I rent another penthouse apartment in Küssnacht am Rigi, primarily to retain a certain proximity to what I consider to be the main centers of Swiss business (Zurich, Basel, Luzern, and Bern).

One mistake I made was to purchase a house in Mont-Sur-Rolle. This was bought in 2006 and sold in 2010. It had a great panoramic view over Lake Geneva and came with a swimming pool and a private vineyard. My

8 Quality of Education, Career, Business, and Art

friend Bjørg was a strong influence when it came to this decision. In retrospect, however, it turned out that maintaining this was too much of a hassle. And my heavy travel schedule at that time made it rather unattractive for Bjørg to live there alone.

As previously alluded to, my sisters and I own a summer house in Ulvøsund in the south of Norway, as well as a hunting property in Salmeli. These properties were inherited from our parents. While these are houses rather than apartments, they are of unique sentimental value to me and are also crucial for maintaining good relationships with my two sisters and in-laws. The two locations are indeed rather unique: finding good shorefront properties is almost impossible today!

Why Live in Switzerland?

You may ask "why live in Switzerland?" Why would a Norwegian citizen settle in this country? As previously discussed, I had obtained teaching positions at IMEDE and later IMD in 1971 and in 1979, respectively. Indeed, it was quite by chance that I got my first taste of living in Switzerland. The area surrounding Lausanne, located on the shore of Lake Geneva, is particularly attractive. When I became President of IMD in 1993, I was contractually obliged to move to Lausanne. I have maintained my ties to this region of Switzerland, even after resigning in 2008.

I had gotten used to living in Switzerland by 2008, but decided to move to the Zurich region, partly because the bulk of Switzerland's business activities seemed to be conducted in that part of the country, and partly also due to the lower taxes. I ended up settling in Küssnacht am Rigi, in Kanton Schwyz. As a keen adversary of complexity and bureaucracy, both in my personal and professional lives, I have come to appreciate the relative lack of bureaucracy in the canton of Schwyz. The simpler the better, and the clearer the better! Also, there is a good climate in Switzerland, with many more daylight hours during the winter season than is the case in my home country of Norway. Plus, the skiing is superb!

So, my preference for living in Switzerland is driven by two overriding factors: first, there is a more equal distribution of daylight hours throughout the year in Switzerland than there is in Norway, due to Switzerland's more southerly location. A friendlier climate prevails. Both Switzerland and Norway have wonderful natural resources—many mountains, forests, lakes, and rivers. Both countries have excellent skiing and enjoy outdoor lifestyles. Second, there seems to be more individual freedom in Switzerland, with perhaps not quite as much central governmental intervention as there is in Norway. Although both countries are socially rather homogenous, with a certain pressure to conform, Switzerland seems to be somewhat more "relaxed." And this latter aspect seems to increase year on year, resulting in more and more foreign residents choosing to live in Switzerland and thus contributing to the further opening up and diversity of the country. Individuals are "invited" to participate in decision-making, especially at the local and regional levels. One largely pays for services as needed, rather than having the government decide this required on one's behalf (health insurance, schooling, church, etc.). However, the benefit for me of living in Switzerland is not so much a matter of "saving," for example, on taxes, but rather a sense of "freedom," such as allowing me as an individual to have more of a say over factors that might affect me.

What about the differences between the various cantons, for example, Schwyz versus Vaud (where Lausanne is located)? Schwyz is very liberal, and there is little bureaucracy. The public sector is a "partner" with its citizens, which is perhaps more easily achieved in a relatively small canton, unlike in a larger canton such as Vaud. Vaud, on the other hand, might thus be described as perhaps semi-socialist and slightly more bureaucratic. Perhaps this is only to be expected, being on the border with France! But Vaud has a more beautiful landscape and is certainly a comfortable place in which to live.

Living in Switzerland does also have its downsides, of course, including being at a distance from my family and friends, particularly my children and grandchildren. But air travel has changed much of that. It is only a very short flight from Zurich to Oslo!

Quality and Business School Curricula

To appreciate business school operations as well as the curricular implications of a focus on quality, let us consider the typical competences of outstanding professors. They often excel in both research and teaching. Research and teaching are "two sides of the same coin" for them. While some professors might be better at one of these tasks than the other, it seems as if a combination of these two is emphasized by most top professors and in the majority of top-of-the-line academic institutions. The criteria for promotion and tenure, as well as bonuses/remunerations, are, however, often skewed toward the research side.

The quality of teaching seems to have suffered in various ways because of this somewhat artificial division between research and teaching. The two have not always been closely connected. Some lecturers may simply not be up to speed when it comes to the latest thinking. Graduate assistants-cum-teachers may lack pedagogical experience in drawing on examples from research. Further, professors who are primarily committed to their research and might have seen teaching as a tedious obligation in the past may no longer be able to get away with such biases in the future. The traditional split between the more prestigious research side and the more quotidian teaching side found in so many academic institutions may not hold up for much longer. Things may be changing!

Past teaching practice in which students are deprived of the excitement of being exposed to more than one avenue of cutting-edge thinking may be no longer acceptable. Good business practice as well as solid curricular design should take this into account, with courses reflecting what the professors in an academic institution can meaningfully deliver, based on both their research competence and their experiences from practical life. A good curriculum should thus not be based on established conventions regarding what learners might expect to find in an academic professor (i.e., mostly research insights), but rather on course content that the professors in an academic institution can teach *well*, reflecting what they are good at and enthusiastic about! Thus, it should be a range of professorial capacities and practical considerations that drive curriculum design. This would ensure higher quality teaching and lessen passivity and boredom, with a blended approach to research and teaching.

How would the business school of the future deal with the basics of each subject area? My sense is that the fundamentals should be delivered virtually, making use of self-study. The key is for the cutting-edge aspects of the curriculum, i.e., research-based content, to be delivered through face-to-face pedagogy. Full priority should be given to delivering a balanced view looking at topics from a number of perspectives. This is the only way to assure quality, in my opinion!

Key Learnings

A keen focus on quality has been a driving force in many aspects of my life, from educational choices, through the career steps I have pursued in business, as well as when it comes to my interest in my art collection, choice of residences, as well as in my all-important relationships with life partners. Important decisions driven by quality considerations have generally turned out well. This quality-driven approach seems to have worked for me!

9

Diversity Is Key!

Why is diversity such a critical aspect of a vision? And why does diversity typically lead to growth? How does a good vision[1] relate to more effective executive education? These are some of the questions I will focus on in this chapter.

A focus on growth is key for most businesses. I will argue in this chapter that growth is more readily achieved through diversity. Looking at phenomena from different angles typically leads us to a better understanding and richer insights and this has been pointed out by many writers, including Bjørnsson who I have previously quoted on this topic. In his essay *Foreigner* (1852), he makes the point that an isolationistic/nationalistic attitude often leads to narrower viewpoints. Lehrer (2009) makes a similar argument but now with a focus on the arts, discussing how eight different types of artists produce complementary views on problems from neuroscience. This is a subject I look at in Chap. 8, in the section on art. Complex processes of the brain seem to become more easily understood by adding perspectives from the arts. And we have seen in numerous examples from history that shifts away from diversity can lead

---

[1] For a good discussion of how to delineate and implement an effective vision, see Konovalov (2021).

© The Author(s), under exclusive license to Springer Nature Switzerland AG 2022
P. Lorange, *Learning and Teaching Business*,
https://doi.org/10.1007/978-3-031-14564-3_9

to narrower, less inspirational thinking, from the decay of France after the expulsion of the Protestant Huguenots in the seventeenth century to Nazi Germany's rout of Jewish intellectuals in the twentieth century and the corresponding loss of preeminence of German academic institutions. The Technical University in Dresden, for instance, used to be one of the preeminent institutions for technical education in Europe, together with ETH in Zurich and Imperial College in London. It then became more or less extinct after World War II. So, it is essential to preserve openness and to avoid dogmatism and isolation, i.e., to think outside the box!

Diversity matters! My own experience confirms this, and I will report on how I have experienced the benefits of diversity in several contexts. As we shall see, not only better decisions but also "better" learning comes about when one draws on many different sources.

Let us, therefore, briefly discuss how diversity as I have experienced it can lead to success within the following four areas: academia, the arts, business, and sport. We will, as a corollary, also see how a lack of diversity can lead to dogmatism and slowdowns in these fields, and elsewhere as well! While I cannot claim to have been centrally involved in every area we will discuss, I have had at least some involvement.

Academia

A story from MIT comes to mind, shared with me by Dr. William Pounds, the former Dean of Sloan School of Management. According to him, many academic disciplines, particularly in fields within the sciences, tend to evolve in a stepwise mode: at times, they may develop rapidly, going from one significant stage to another, then remaining more or less stagnant, often over relatively long periods of time, analogous to the landings one finds on a staircase. Optics is one such field, which remained quite stagnant for a long period of time, only to then evolve rapidly following the introduction of new laser-driven insights. In order to introduce a steadier rate of progression, it now aims to add new disciplinary elements to stagnant areas, i.e., to try to introduce diversity on a more or less ongoing basis.

Here are three other examples from academia. Over the last few decades, there seems to have been a very strong propensity for many academic institutions to use mathematical tools to handle business-related issues. Examples of this can be found in what is typically labelled "operations research" when it comes to both research and teaching at institutions such as the Norwegian School of Economics and Business Administration (NHH), Yale, and MIT's Sloan School of Management, as well as at many other institutions. The problem with this seems to be that it has led to "too many solutions to the same challenge," perhaps at the expense of variety. Over time, significant parts of the output using this approach end up lacking in originality. A lack of diversity thus has taken its toll! It should be noted, however, that this relatively unilateral and extreme focus on mathematical tools now seems to be on the wane.

Much of the research methodology that has now become mainstream stems predominantly from Karl Popper's hypothesis testing approach (Popper, 1935), the so-called "null-hypotheses." However, this might have led to a degree of sterility when it comes to published research outputs. Much of what is being published in academic journals today, for instance, seems rather dull. Perhaps dogmatism has driven out eclectic originality, at least to some extent?

My final example is drawn from HBS and this school's tradition of extensive use of the so-called case method in its teaching (Towl, 1969). Here too, originality and creativity might seem to have suffered, perhaps due to some unintentional dogmatism about the preferred mode of teaching. Teaching seemed to have become less inspiring! Perhaps variety is missing?

Why is it that so much of the output from academia is becoming so unexciting, boring even? This seems to be true for much of the research as well as the teaching taking place in many of our higher institutions of learning. My sense is that strong "bridges" are key to ameliorating this; bridges between academia and business, between learning and practice, between education and execution. Institutions need to strive for dynamism and boldness, even to be revolutionary at times! Variety is important, just as we have seen in the case of the arts.

Research

Following on from this broader discussion about the need for diversity in academia, let us now look at this issue in some detail in relation to the sub-area of research. I will cite four examples, several of which I have had some degree of involvement in.

A good example of how eclecticism in research bears fruit can be found at NHH in the business area of shipping, where academicians trained as economists have worked in parallel with economic historians, all focused on shipping strategies and markets. The result is an exceptionally original and creative body of outputs (Tenold, 2018). I had the privilege to participate in some of the early research efforts here (Lorange & Norman, 1973).

An example of eclecticism in leadership comes from Harvard University, from its renowned School of Architecture. The Dean in charge came from "across the river," namely from HBS, and his field of specialization was not architecture, but operations management. His name was Dr. Maurice Kilbridge, and he had been trained at the University of Chicago. A quest for eclecticism was thereby met, which in the end further enhanced the preeminence of the school. Eclecticism in academic leadership research is a topic that many, including me, have worked on extensively (Lorange, 2019b).

Let us now return to IMD. Family business is taught and researched hand in hand with the school's other disciplines, most notably finance, strategy, and organizational behavior. The result seems to be an exceptionally vibrant family business program, well exemplified by outputs focusing on family philanthropy (Vogel, 2020). My family and I have been involved in these efforts (Lorange, 2019a), and IMD has established an endowed professorial chair in my name in family business and entrepreneurship. Eclecticism in practice!

Let us consider a Spanish university in Madrid, *Instituto de Empresa* (IE). IE started out as a business school but has since expanded to include a law school, architecture school, and engineering school. A widespread use of digital technology is a common denominator, evident today with a considerable investment in the school's WOW Room[2] as well as extensive mobile virtual technology experiences. IE's top leadership team claim that this has been a key factor in attracting a wide array of talented students as well as a strong faculty. Diversity seems to be at the heart of this successful private university, a key factor in an impressive evolutionary path (Lorange, 2019b). It should be noted that several other business schools are now adopting similar approaches. IMD in Lausanne, for instance, is offering successful educational programs this way.

Curriculum Design

While I will return to effective curriculum design in the concluding chapter (Chap. 16), I should stress a few issues here relative to the application of diversity and eclecticism in the design of effective curricula in business schools.

NHH The curriculum of this institution certainly reflected diversity. A student might choose two electives from a wide range of subjects, including different languages, geography, history, and mathematics. Further, the predominantly economics-driven curriculum has dealt with topics specific to the firm as well as more society-focused elements. A deliberate strive to enhance diversity has always prevailed, however.

Undergraduate Programs in US Colleges: Harvard, Yale, and University of Pennsylvania The curriculum choices of these academic institutions are rooted in their arts and sciences departments. If a student decides, for instance, to concentrate on a particular field within the arts, such as a language, then he/she must also enroll in other courses from different disciplines, including options from the humanities, such as history, as well as from social science (psychology, economics, political science, etc.), and a course in the sciences. A belief in diversity is the driver here!

---

[2] This is an auditorium where each student participates remotely, and where each is seen by the others on his/her own individual screen.

Yale, Doctoral Programs Students in various fields are also required to acquire proficiency in a language, either German or French.

The Lauder Institute at Wharton and the University of Pennsylvania A student must take both the standard MBA curriculum (from Wharton) as well as qualify for an MA in one of eight language options (from the University of Pennsylvania's School of Arts and Science). Diversity is used to create leaders who can succeed in the international sphere!

Harvard Business School's Doctoral Program Students have traditionally had to pass an exam in "The Administrative Point of View," where they had to demonstrate a capability to deal with real-life business problems. While there are no specific courses to prepare students for this exam, the many case discussions found in almost all classes at HBS provide adequate preparation, perhaps. It should also be noted that the MBA students in HBS's famous program must also submit around 25 so-called WAC reports (Written Analysis Cases), thus providing training in putting key eclecticism-inspired analysis to paper.

In conclusion, it seems vital to incorporate variety into a modern business school's curricula. This stands in stark contrast to university-level studies in many other fields, particularly in Europe, where students are typically expected to specialize from day one of their studies. My recommendation is the opposite. Good learning tends to be based on deliberate diversity. Good curriculum design should reflect this!

The Arts

Art is another area in which eclecticism seems to make a difference. I have experienced this in my capacity as an active arts collector. Let us briefly discuss two examples from the arts.

We are all quite familiar with different types of galleries, where paintings, sculptures, and artistic installations are routinely exhibited. Some museums specialize in one artist, such as the famous Munch Museum in Oslo, or the Van Gogh Museum in Amsterdam. Often, however, museums feature multitudes of artists, such as the Louvre in Paris, the Tate in London, the Louisiana in Denmark, or Oslo's Stenersen Museum or

National Museum. At least to their visitors, the latter group offers a much stronger sense of experiencing a wider sense of the creative aspects of art. We, the public, and this includes me, feel the benefits of such eclecticism. I am currently exploring ways to expose the public to my own art collection, where a diversity of focus, rather than specialization is a key aspect.

Let us consider the Verbier Festival of Classical Music. Here, musicians young *and* old from *many* different nationalities come together to perform. There is a wide *variety* of music and composers are "delivered" in different physical settings. The effect, once again, is that the audience has a better experience thanks to the power of eclecticism!

Business

I will provide several examples to illustrate the power of eclecticism in business. First, let us consider an Oslo-based firm within the field of financial services, *Pareto*. This company is engaged in a variety of services, mostly what we would classify as financial services (ventures, syndication, banking, insurance, stock brokerage, etc.), but also, with activities in other marketplaces, such as real estate, ship brokerage, and travel. The company has offices in various cities in Scandinavia as well as in Germany and Switzerland. Its employees come from many countries and professions. The main common denominator seems to be that all employees must have as a minimum an understanding of finance and numbers! The result is that this exceptional diversity has led to exceptional performance. Many clients, including SUI, have benefited significantly from this. For SUI, this has in particular allowed our firm to participate in several innovative shipping projects in which we have invested.

I would also highlight the Oslo-based *Mesterbygg* Group which is active in real estate. This firm is part of the Oslo-based privately owned business portfolio group, *Ferd*. *Mesterbrygg* is active in many areas, including in land development, home construction, and marketing of properties. Its parent, *Ferd*, is also Scandinavia's largest provider of building materials and paints. Further, the group successfully utilizes web-based sales and distribution channels. Having been able to develop such a diverse business model seems to be related to the fact that the firm has an exceptionally creative organization. I experienced this creativity in person when the Board of Christiania Eiendomsselskap, a firm partly owned by SUI, negotiated a deal with Mesterbygg for the latter to acquire an option to build on a piece of land belonging to Christiania Eiendomsselskap.

Moving now to the large Copenhagen-based ship owning *A.P. Möller-Maersk Group*, active not only in shipping but also in logistics and, until recently, in oil. The legendary Mr. Maersk McKinney Möller was the majority owner and CEO, a position he held for 52 years! Mr. Möller deliberately built strengths into his company based on diversity. Not only was his firm involved in many aspects of shipping, i.e., tankers, bulk carriers, car carriers, offshore supply ships of various types, and, of course, container ships (18% world market share and the world's largest operator until taken over by Geneva-based MSC in 2021), it was also a major owner and operator of harbors specializing in container ship loading and unloading. Until recently his firm was also active in offshore oil exploration (North Sea, Middle East, etc.). Finally, the company used to be the largest shareholder in *Dankse Bank*, allowing it to "cherry pick" exceptional finance talents from there. His firm further used to own 50% of *Danish Supermarkets*, so that exceptional marketing talents might be identified and hired. As noted, the company owned a large shipyard, *Lindöe*, allowing the group to deliver new ships with innovative designs in order to obtain a benefit from this up to a year ahead of the competition! Diversity clearly seems to have driven their success. I had the privilege to discuss all of this with Mr. McKinney Möller on several occasions. In line with this tradition, the current chairperson of the company is Jim Hagemann Snabe, formerly co-CEO of SAP and now also chairperson of Siemens, while the shipping trained Sören Skov is the CEO, i.e., diversity at work.

We can see the power of diversity in venture firms such as Berkshire Hathaway (Warren Buffett, CEO) or EQT (Christian Sinding, CEO). Both firms are highly diversified, and while it is perhaps not so diverse in its competence mix at the corporate level, the top team receives a wide array of inputs from its various investments. The same can perhaps be said about my family's portfolio investment firm, S. Ugelstad Invest (SUI) (Lorange, 2019a, 2019b). While SUI's corporate team is very small, a positive effect comes from a diversity of inputs from the more than 40 investments in which SUI is involved, again building on eclecticism.

Sports

There are several aspects of the various sports I have enjoyed that have contributed to the development of my thinking, particularly when it comes to the benefits of teamwork, perseverance, and of broadening one's horizons. At the outset, I should stress that I do not see myself as a particularly athletic type. I broke my left leg ski-jumping at the age of 11, which led me to having to be in a plaster cast for 6 months. Later, I played a great deal of tennis (there is a tennis court at our family's summer house in Ulvøsund). I was coached by the late Mr. Jan O. Gundersen. He "pushed" me in a beneficial way! I also did a lot of alpine skiing, initially in the Pocono Mountains, Vermont, and later in Verbier and at Kvitfjell. A key learning from this was the power of good coordination! I also enjoy walking and still do to this day. For me, sport brings fulfillment, requiring goal setting and discipline. Learning that it takes this type of peace of mind to think clearly was key. It can also add healthy routines to a daily or weekly schedule. I have enjoyed both individual sports as well as team sports, and I have benefitted from inspiration from both.

Sailing has played a prominent part in my life. My first sailboat was a BB-11, a gift from my Uncle Rolf. I learnt to sail in this boat, which had a crew of two, in addition to me at the helm. I started to realize the power of small teams and diversity! One day in 1958, outside Hankö, in heavy winds, at the age of 15 with my father also onboard, we took in a lot of water and almost crashed into another BB-11. It was certainly scary. I felt out of control! Partly, this was due to the water flowing into the boat at such a rapid rate. Partly also, I was uncertain about the rules that should be followed in such an emergency. What I had drilled into my head did not necessarily seem to apply! There was little coordination between my father and me. We both had different competences and strengths. Teamwork, drawing on our diverse competences, might have come in useful to cope with this crisis. A key learning here was how to cope with crises.

Later, I moved into sailing single-handed Finn dinghies. The power of learning how to sail entirely on my own became clearer now. I participated in Finn Gold Cups (World Championships), but with unimpressive results. In the Kieler Woche and later in the Nordic Championship in Helsinki, however, I had some modest successes. I was competing single-handedly for many years and was fully supported by my parents in this. While being alone, I definitely had to develop a broad-mindedness, a "diversity of mind."

I also learnt a lot from being a member of a large sailing team (11 people) crewing the *Norseman*, owned and skippered by my father. This was all about "we, we, we"! I enjoyed working with the crew as well as with my father and learned several key lessons from him, perhaps above all the power of meticulous preparation and understanding critical success factors. The best equipment does matter and there should be no excess weight onboard. Whether we like it or not, competing in the top league implies that one must be ready and willing to invest time and money. It can be expensive! The role of a firm boss, in this case my father, is important.

The experience of being part of a successful team might in part be compared to what we call having "skin in the game" when it comes to participating in business projects, not only as actors but also on the ownership side. Here, we had to train, invest time, live together, and become committed. Having skin in the game is equally important in sport.

One of my major weaknesses is a relative lack of technical skills. This was not only evidenced when I practiced various sports myself, but also when it comes to using many of the day-to-day amenities offered by modern electronics, such as mobile phones, the Internet, and laptops. But perhaps I am not good at using these gadgets because of a lack of interest! I do not want such tasks to "distract" me! Assistance from great personal associates (Kari Nergaard, Heidi Brown, Lizzie Schwegler-Ellis, Eva Ferrari, Anette Polzer, Patricia Bahr, Karin Mugnaini, and Leda Nishino) have "bailed me out" on many occasions! A key lesson seems to be that while many individuals might be open to diversity and eclecticism, this can sometimes only be achieved by drawing on the skills of others.

It would be impossible for me to conclude this section on sports without referring to the fascinating book *The Boys in the Boat* by Daniel James Brown (2013), recommended to me by the CEO of Victorinox, Mr. Carl Elsener. This book chronicles the American crew of eight rowing boat legendary Olympic gold medal win at the Berlin Olympics in 1936. The boat crossed the finish line a few feet ahead of Italy with Germany in third place, with Hitler watching from the grandstand. An incredible level of dedication, team spirit, and a sense of loyalty between the crew members lay behind this win. This is one of the most inspiring but incredible undertakings in sports history, in my opinion, and for me an eye-opening read.

Key Learnings

Diversity matters! It tends to enhance performance. This seems to be a fundamental truth. I have always tried to take advantage of this realization. Openness—being "connected" with other complementary "resource" individuals—is, of course, a precondition. Diversity only works when people want it to work! Mutual respect, a willingness to be humble, keeping an open mind, strong listening capabilities, and a willingness to give more than one takes are all key here. All this adds up to being ready and willing to put in the necessary effort to succeed!

10

The Importance of Managing Risk and Uncertainty

Pabrai (2007) suggests a useful distinction between risk and uncertainty: risk measures the value of an asset as of the present, thereby including historical developments as they relate to a given asset (such as exposure to disasters, whether these are underlying values that might not have been fully reflected in an asset's price, such as steel prices when a ship is scrapped and values of various assets that might be spun off). Uncertainty, in contrast, measures how an asset's value is likely to fare in the future, such as expected appreciations in the stock market and shipping rates in the future. A good aim for the successful investor might be to search for assets that enjoy low risk combined with a high degree of uncertainty. Many investors, as well as a multitude of analysts, tend to make relatively little distinction between risk and uncertainty. They, at times, equate these concepts with each other, or at best take a somewhat blurred approach. In contrast, a clear delineation between risk and uncertainty should be a precondition for successful investing and asset management. Pabrai calls this "Dhandho Investing" (2007).

It is difficult, in fact, almost impossible for profits to be generated through good investment decisions or to see how favorable outcomes from business decisions, in general, might be made, without having to

© The Author(s), under exclusive license to Springer Nature Switzerland AG 2022
P. Lorange, *Learning and Teaching Business*,
https://doi.org/10.1007/978-3-031-14564-3_10

take some risk and managing uncertainty. As Merckelback says, "taking some risk is necessary to make money" (Merckelback, 2020). The question is therefore to decide on how much risk one is willing to take. Given that there might be a business opportunity with a potentially good return on the horizon, how much might one be ready to invest and in which project? It should be noted that considerable efforts are often made by investors to find projects with lower risks with a potentially favorable upside (high uncertainty), thereby enjoying relatively high returns (see Pabrai, 2007).

In the following section, I review a number of ways of identifying projects with relatively low risk, all of which I have practiced at SUI. I also highlight some of the cases where mistakes were made. There have not only been successes, of course! All examples come from various commercial activities in which I have been involved. Much of what we will discuss will be relevant in other settings too. Finding projects that are undervalued, i.e., that offer relatively low risk, is usually not sufficient on its own. There should also be the prospect of exceptionally good increases in future value for a particular project, i.e., relatively high uncertainty. This dimension must also be managed.

Due Diligence

It is, of course, critical to undertake a thorough due diligence analysis. There are five considerations that are particularly critical in my opinion and in the light of my experience:

* The revenue side. Are customers likely to buy this offering, and at the proposed price?
* The need for capital. How much capital is now needed to run the business? Is this so-called "burn rate" reasonable? Is there a realistic likelihood of reaching break-even, and how far into the future might this take place?
* The competition. Who else is operating in this business space? How are they likely to respond? How vulnerable might we then be?

10 The Importance of Managing Risk and Uncertainty   113

- The entrepreneur behind a proposed project. What is his/her track record? Is he/she putting in liquidity of their own, i.e., does he/she have "skin-in-the-game"? Is he/she likely to be able to take rapid, decisive, ameliorating corrective actions if needed? In short, does he/she have a reputation for a certain level of dynamism?
- Is there a reasonable likelihood that the proposed asset will accrue at a reasonable rate? For instance, are we faced with a situation where we are buying when market cycles seem to be on the low side, with a relatively high likelihood of an increase in the relevant market cycle, i.e., is there a "buy low, sell high" situation? Is there relatively high uncertainty?

At SUI, we made several mistakes when it comes to due diligence. Sloppy, hastily done due diligence has cost SUI dearly. In particular, this can often be traced back to believing in what we were told by a project's proposer, including what was written in often glorified investment prospectuses, rather than undertaking sufficient *independent* up-front checks of our own. Here are some of SUI's worst mistakes:

- A vacation home project in Bulgaria. Here the initial building lot on the Black Ocean coast slid into the Black Sea and was lost. While this was dramatic, there was thankfully no loss of life. In the wake of the immediate shock, we decided to build the vacation home on another piece of land, located around one kilometer from the beach. Although it was in a beautiful location, it turned out to be too far from the oceanfront. The project was a failure. Our assessment regarding the uncertainty associated with this project turned out to be wrong: the future upside was simply not there!
- A-Beauty. SUI invested too early and too much in a Zurich-based beauty salon/beauty products concept. We had relied too heavily on the proposer's assessment. This in part had to do with the good impression I had gotten from the proposer at an earlier stage, when he was a consultant at the Lorange Institute. It resulted in failure. Our assessment of the risk was wrong. In particular, the project's burn rate was too high! Expenses were out of control. Several of the key persons involved turned out to be too weak!

* Reebate. This Germany-based project was given too high a valuation. The manager in charge did not seem to be sufficiently alert to the need to make quick downward adjustments to reduce the burn rate. His prior experience had been with much larger, well-financed firms, and not with start-ups. Our assessment of both risks as well as the management was wrong, and the project never became a good value proposition.

As an investor, one must, of course, take the responsibility for failures such as these. There will almost always be unexpected adverse factors that one might point to in retrospect, but this is no excuse. In the end, it is solely the decision maker who is responsible for the misjudgments. I have learnt a lot about this from Peter Brabeck, the former CEO of Nestlé and a long-term board member of IMD, particularly when it comes to handling failure (Brabeck, 2020). I acknowledge that sharing can lead to new insights and learning, a key to progress!

Due diligence also applies to many other areas. For instance, I had the privilege to be part of an accreditation panel from AMBA (Association of MBA degree-offering schools) and visited several business schools located in the central China area. Each school had prepared detailed documentation beforehand. Their leading faculty members and administrators also gave presentations. There was a lot for me to internalize. I did have a relatively good understanding of how business schools should function, based on my many years of experience both as a faculty member as well as a senior administrator of several pre-eminent business schools. My conclusion was that while all these institutions had made serious preparations, I was still not inclined to vote in favor of their accreditation. It was my duty and responsibility to raise my concerns. Thorough due diligence was not only called for, but it also made me skeptical!

Thorough due diligence typically calls for *both* good industrial insight *as well as* a willingness and ability to make the effort of going through large amounts of documentation and forecasts. While experience might now and then somewhat ameliorate preparation, it is nevertheless largely a matter of internalizing facts, i.e., undertaking systematic analysis. In the end, it usually comes down to whether the price is reasonable for a particular investment that has been assessed through due diligence. Is the

10 The Importance of Managing Risk and Uncertainty

project properly priced? As previously noted, buying on the low side, going low risk, is only half of the equation. It is equally important to sell on the high side to enjoy the benefits from increases in valuation. Taking advantage of underlying cyclicality is often key here. This has become a major driver for SUI in choosing proper timing for exits. And this helps to reduce risk! *Good timing* tends to be one of SUI's core competences! Having a clear understanding of when and how to exit from a project is an important element of proper due diligence.

One approach that we have followed at SUI is to rely on individuals and organizations with more experience in a particular field than us, and perhaps who have more time to do detailed due diligence analysis than we do. We have had good experiences with two types of entities when it comes to this:

* Participation in funds (Norges Investor, ICON Capital, NCA Search Fund, Sole Shipping Fund, Storm Bond Fund, Jockey Fund, Serendipity Fund). Here the fund manager is responsible for due diligence.
* Participation in search funds (RCG, Antler, Varro), where, similarly, the manager in charge is not only responsible for due diligence but is an investor as well ("skin in the game").

We have also worked closely with other investors with strong reputations and track records. Two such individuals that I have enjoyed co-investing with are Mr. Egil Bodd and Dr. Paul Eckbo. Both are smart, creative, and insightful. It makes it easier for me to do due diligence. Investing when there are strong co-investors is thus key for SUI. This was also the case for SUI's investment in the Stockholm-based pharmaceuticals firm, *Affibody*, where Ingvar Kamprad (IKEA) and the Wallenberg Group also participated as investors. Due diligence was relatively easy for SUI to do here. Being "alone" as a key investor in a project, in contrast, typically calls for more thorough due diligence.

It goes without saying that SUI always avoids investing more than is necessary to secure a meaningful position in a project. Calls for additional capital at a later date might imply dilution of our initial ownership share. This was, for instance, the case with Oslo-based software firm

116   P. Lorange

Keystone, which merged with a Swedish competitor, resulting in a dilution of SUI's ownership share to ca. 2.5% from our initial 5% ownership. It was nevertheless a good investment! Further, SUI always tries to avoid very small so-called "listening post" investments. Following up on too many small investments can take as much time as when larger sums are invested. A key learning for SUI is to pay particularly close attention to when there are other strong investors involved, and to try to better understand what they are doing; another aspect of proper due diligence. A strategy of being a "close follower" can often be the best approach.

Properly managing one's risk thus calls for a reasonable degree of diversification as well as a prudent due diligence process. I have come to believe that there are at least two core considerations related to making prudent decisions; namely, deciding how much to invest, and focusing on a possible exit right from the moment the decision is made to get in. I will now discuss each of these in turn.

How Much Should We Invest?

As already noted, experience has taught me not to invest too heavily in a project at the outset, but rather to carefully monitor initial progress, investing more at later stages if required. I recognize that this may mean that certain investments end up being relatively costlier later on, but I am generally willing to incur such opportunity losses in order to better manage the uncertainty. Good examples of this are SUI's investments in Antler, or in the Jockey Fund, both with gradually increasing investment commitments from SUI as the market values of these funds increased. A poor example is Sargas, where SUI committed too many resources upfront and ended up taking a significant loss. Here, we took too high a risk. There was simply not enough realistic market upside. Coincidentally, it should be noted, however, that SUI was able to recoup some of its losses at a much later date when a Swedish subsidiary of Sargas which had taken over many of Sargas' technology-based patents went public. The patience that we showed by converting our debt to the Swedish subsidiary to equity paid off in the end. But we were lucky indeed! So, mitigating risk is key, by not going in too early with too many resources.

How Early Should One Invest?

I have never been a so-called "angel investor." I am not a start-up expert. For me, a project should ideally have an established revenue track, as well as a solid customer base. If not, then the risk tends to be too high. I have, however, deviated from this basic principle several times, for instance, when investing in two medical ventures in pre-diagnostics and prevention focused on Alzheimer's disease, but only with small ownership shares of 2.5% and 3.13%, respectively.

Taking Profits

I have come to believe that consideration should be given to how one will exit from an investment from the very start. My experience also tells me to try to take profits whenever possible, by selling out a part of a given project, for example, to enjoy further value accrual from what remains of the investment, more or less as a "free ticket." For instance, SUI more than doubled what we invested in two container ships by selling part of our ownership, ending up with a significantly smaller investment in the two ships more or less for free, at low risk. Ultimately, we reinvested the proceeds in a chemical tanker project. Taking profits to gradually reduce exposure and thus also risk has often been a successful way at SUI.

Key Learnings

Taking risks is part of the game, and is not bad per se, as long as there is an opportunity for a significant future upside, i.e., significant uncertainty. It is unwise to take unnecessarily high risks, however, especially when there is little or no expected upside later on. In this chapter, we discussed several ways in which we at SUI are attempting to manage risk and uncertainty. The general takeaway is that it is realistic to be able to manage risk and to take advantage of uncertainty—up to a point. Carrying out a proper due diligence process is perhaps the most critical element here. To do this realistically is perhaps the most significant management challenge when it comes to articulating what successful entrepreneurship is.

Underpinning the discussion in this chapter is the premise that risk and uncertainty can more easily be managed when a corporation is a portfolio rather than a so-called heritage business. In the latter case, the business could be vulnerable to a slew of potentially negative factors, including macroeconomic swings in the business, competitive shifts among established competitors, new governmental regulations in the industry in which it operates, or "disruptive" new entrants (Christensen, 2013). A key learning for me has been that a balanced portfolio is critical to managing risks and uncertainties. So, what are some of the implications of coping with risk and uncertainty for running businesses and academic institutions, as well as for curriculum design? A student needs to learn how to recognize risks, as well as how to ameliorate these.

Perhaps a key distinction when it comes to risk versus uncertainty might be illustrated by contrasting the *raison d'êtres* of each of the two leading Swiss business schools, IMI (in Geneva) and IMEDE (in Lausanne), which eventually merged to become IMD. IMI used to put a lot of emphasis on the analysis of various macro-issues to come up with key insights regarding major risks. IMEDE, on the other hand, seemed to focus primarily on various smaller details about how firms made decisions, to better understand the inherent uncertainties. Neither of the two institutions was entirely "correct," however, in that both were coping with only certain parts of the realities of the business world. However, merging the two schools, to gain a fuller focus for teaching about business and creating a more realistic curriculum where both macro-agenda-orientated issues and micro-agenda issues were taught led to a better understanding of things. An "ideal" business or academic focus, and a curriculum for an academic institution of the future must include both foci—macro and micro—so as to be able to effectively cope with both risk and uncertainty!

11

Discipline and Integrity in Decision-Making

This chapter discusses a set of issues related to decision-making requiring both discipline and integrity, both critical topics for the running of any institution, including a business school curriculum. While most of us are normally relatively clear when it comes to the limits we should not step over, there are unfortunately plenty of examples of decisions that we might describe as essentially being "shades of grey" (Brennan, 2016). Decisions might, for instance, be unethical but nonetheless legal. We might think about commodity traders here, whose practices might at times be unethical but still legal (Blas & Farchy, 2021). To illustrate how to cope with these types of issues in relation to both business, academic management, and curriculum design, I will discuss how a few of these "shades of grey" decisions have been dealt with in my own experience.

Decision-making relies on combining relatively objective facts with one's own experience. The quality of this experience is important, above all built through a combination of a determination to reach specific targets as well as reflective learning; looking back and learning from what might have occurred. We shall discuss this in the final chapter of this book. For now, it suffices to say that there should be a *blend* of rational and subjective thinking.

© The Author(s), under exclusive license to Springer Nature Switzerland AG 2022
P. Lorange, *Learning and Teaching Business*,
https://doi.org/10.1007/978-3-031-14564-3_11

I always strive to find seemingly objective inputs into a decision, based on verifiable data. But intuition and experience also clearly play a role. Over time, I have developed relatively good intuition, both when it comes to business and academia. But this has clearly not always been the case! Learning from one's failures is key. Analysis typically takes time. There are no shortcuts!

My thinking about this seems to coincide with the conclusions drawn by several prominent decision-making scholars, such as Simon (1992), with his concept of bounded rationality, and Lehrer (2010), with his focus on decisions as a finely tuned blend of both subjective feeling and rational reason. A more precise mix here will depend on the situation, of course.

Examples of Focused Decision-Making

Decision-making is thus a *combination of* analysis and intuition. SUI's decision in 2000 to invest in two small bulk carriers capable of travelling through the docks of the St. Lawrence seaways illustrates this. The *rational* analytics consisted largely of interrogating reports from the Boston-based market intelligence forecasting firm, Marsoft. The reports forecasted a positive outlook for handy-size bulk carriers at the time. But I had also *judgmental* inputs to add. During my years on the Board of the Shipowners Olsen & Ugelstad (O&U), I had become quite familiar with this company's liner operations on the Great Lakes/St. Lawrence seaway (Fjell Line). So, my intuition "told" me to enter this shipping segment, but with larger, more effective bulk carriers from O&U's smaller, more traditional liner ships. Rational analysis and intuition came together, and a decision to go for these two bulk carriers was made. It turned out to be a good decision!

Discipline is an essential part of maintaining focus. At S. Ugelstad Invest (SUI), we try to exclusively purchase assets that seem "solid." Specifically, we always assess the profiles of the individual promoters behind a proposed investment project. Is his/her track record solid and relevant? Is his/her "chemistry" right for us: will we be comfortable working with this person? In the end, it comes down to discipline in decision-making here too.

Hard work is another vital element. Twice a year, when I was President at both BI and later at IMD, I conducted formal face-to-face reviews with each faculty member. Each review consisted of a 1-h discussion, which involved a large amount of preparation on my part, including reviewing reading that each faculty member had submitted beforehand.

From an "analytical" point of view, I had the specific *outputs* of each individual faculty member to consider. The complementary inputs involved what might be considered the *quality* of these various inputs, based primarily on my experience. It was hard work to arrive at a synthesis, based on a combination of analytical and judgmental inputs, giving feedback, and deciding on bonuses, or even (rare) terminations. This required discipline, and it was hard work!

Targeting

Setting and aiming for targets is always key. This might typically entail a mix of shorter- *and* longer-term foci, a combination of "gut feeling" and analysis.

In 2006, I made the decision to sell SUR. At the time, I tried to determine the optimum time for the actual exit. Behaviorally, I felt an obligation to discuss this with key members of staff, both ashore as well as the senior officers on the ships. Their input was universally negative. Exiting did not seem to make sense to them. SUR's traditions weighed heavily. It might also, of course, have had to do with a desire to safeguard their jobs. For me, the status quo did not make good sense. Capturing good economic value was crucial for me. Thus, I initiated a process of outsourcing head office functions, thereby reducing staff numbers. Some 4 years later, when the relevant PSV market cycle seemed to peak again, I was able to sell, without encountering the same staff resistance. The *long-term* target—to exit—was finally achieved through a combination of "rational" analysis (regarding the market cycle) *and* behavioral instincts (organizational considerations, emotions), but now among a much smaller group of executives.

Being reflective is an important part of this story. All the reactions gathered from various stakeholders regarding the sale of SUR could be seen as helpful: they helped me to process my decision to exit, which took a relatively longer time than the subsequent decision to negotiate a sale. It required a lot of reflection on my part to get to grips with all of this.

Another key attribute for success is to be well organized. There always seems to be a shortage of time when it comes to making decisions about one's business. There is often a relatively short window of opportunity. I would go as far as saying that being well organized is a *precondition* for much good decision-making, allowing time for proper analysis, which can then be combined with one's own judgment and intuition. As noted in Chap. 10, there were at least three occasions on which we failed to do good due diligence, all with negative consequences for SUI. The first is related to SUI's investment in a Zurich-based company that sold cosmetic products and owned clinical beauty shops, where the sales forecasts that were presented to me were taken as read, without much independent checking on our part with prospective customers or by examining competitors. There was little-to-no objective analysis and a lot of subjective judgments. The result was not good. The second example was the German software company providing consumer discounts on products sold in supermarkets. Here too there were no market data that turned out to be good. We carried out no independent analysis and I did not check the track record of the manager in charge, either. When the firm's cash burn rate needed adjusting, he seemed to react too late and too slowly. This ended in the failure of this firm. The third example is the Bulgaria-based vacation home project, where we did not sufficiently check the commercial attractiveness of the facility's location. The learning, in all cases, is that one should *always* apply a thorough analysis *and* check relevant facts. If one's analysis is incomplete, things can easily go wrong.

There are of course many approaches to accumulating insights about discipline in decision-making. One way might be to clearly specify upfront the business areas in which one intends to be active. For example, SUI focuses on the following sectors:

* Stocks and bonds
* Shipping

11 Discipline and Integrity in Decision-Making   123

- Real estate
- Ventures and private equity
- Education

This allows us to better understand what elements of decision-making to focus on for each of these businesses.

Examples of Challenges to Honesty and Integrity

Honest Signaling In reality, SUI, my family business, is relatively small and privately owned. My reputation in academia, academic leadership, and business might, to some degree, positively impact on SUI's image. But it would not be ethical for me to give signals to others that might suggest that SUI is stronger than it actually is.

Sticking to One's Word Most of us like to think that the promises we make will ultimately be honored. When SUI invested in Novelty Food, A-Beauty, and Reebate, the promoters might have mistakenly gotten the perception that SUI would be ready to invest further, quite independently of SUI's management team's assessment of how well the actual projects were developing. Promoters may have felt that we promised this! When projects later ran into problems, the promoters were "surprised" that SUI was not ready to invest more but would rather "face up to the losses" instead. *Implicitly*, these promoters might have been counting on SUI for more support. In order to avoid such unfortunate misunderstandings, it might be wise to invest only when there are several other strong investors involved, i.e., follow-on investments by several investors in parallel; even better, if there is some form of understanding between the investors to coordinate future investments.

Honest Feedback It is important to try to avoid being "nice" when giving feedback and to always focus on the facts. Giving feedback based on the viewpoints of "the last person in one's office" can also be a bad move. As far as possible, feedback should emphasize positive factors, to motivate and encourage individuals to stretch themselves.

When I was president of the Norwegian School of Business (BI), and later of IMD, I gave feedback to faculty members twice a year based on reviews of how each individual had performed. It was important to base such feedback on the actual performance/milestones achieved by each faculty member and *not* on mere promises or random targets-in-progress. It was important to give feedback that *encouraged* better research, stronger teaching, and more meaningful "citizenship" efforts.

Exits It is, of course, a legitimate goal to work toward an exit from a given project. However, we might at times be faced with good governance dilemmas here, with investors perhaps acting in their own interests rather than in the interest of all shareholders.

For example, a leading merchant bank had been assigned to sell a large block of shares in a publicly-traded Danish shipping firm. The research department of this bank analyzed this stock and concluded with a positive "buy" recommendation. SUI then bought some of the stock, largely based on the recommendation. At the same time, however, the trading department of the bank sold a large block of shares that it had been mandated to dispose of, and the stock price predictably dropped. The bank stressed that its research department and its trading department were operating totally independent of each other, with no manipulation of the stock price. I had a hard time believing this, however. So-called "Chinese walls" that are stipulated by the law in such banks may in reality be rather thin!

There are clearly strong ethical concerns when it comes to so-called insider trading. Here, the law is also clear. Such activities are illegal! However, there may also be "shades of grey" if, for example, someone with a significant ownership holding is also on the board of the firm in question. Not only might persons in such insider positions be able to spot whether a firm's shares are on the up or, conversely, running into trouble, they might also be tempted to purchase or sell more shares. A board member may also have an early indication of potential mergers, which might also significantly increase the value of the stock. All such transactions are illegal, however.

There are therefore so-called "lock-up" periods for board members. When I was a board member of the Vancouver-based ship owning firm Seaspan, for instance, I was not legally allowed to trade any of my shares

11 Discipline and Integrity in Decision-Making   125

until specific "trading windows" came about, independent of any major announcements. Practically speaking, however, there turned out to be almost no such "windows," regrettably. Being a board member had its downsides!

Shareholder agreements can come in handy to regulate changes in ownership. SUR owned a little more than 25% in a limited partnership, Federal Navigation, owning the two handy-size bulk carriers specially built for the St. Lawrence seaway. Together with our longstanding partner in Aalesund, J. Hagenaes & Co., we had so-called negative control in the firm, meaning that we could stop (or initiate) efforts to sell assets. However, when our partner then sold his shares to Federal Navigation without informing SUR, this significantly reducing the value of SUR's holding, since there was no longer negative control.

I would like to offer one final example of a potential dilemma, in this case regarding exits by some shareholders, at which time other shareholders might offer to purchase shares. In the late summer of 2021, Mr. Bodd, Mr. Thorleifsson (Board Chairman), and SUI made an offer to the remaining shareholders in Deltager, a Norwegian events services firm, to purchase their shares. The offer received only limited acceptance, however. Several shareholders believed that there might be "something more to come" which might further increase the value of the firm. This was not the case, and there was no further offer on the table, however.

Value Profile

At SUI, as well as in the various other organizational entities that I have been involved with, I have always attempted to maintain an impeccable ethical profile, to make decisions that are in line with this. This might involve staying away from certain businesses, for example, recreational drugs or microfinancing, as well as avoiding doing business with certain individuals with controversial reputations! In general, it is important to try to be consistent here, to build up a good reputation, and to try to avoid questionable business initiatives. The well-publicized Enron saga comes to mind here. This company was reporting impressive growth, both in sales as well as in profitability. Many business schools made use of

Enron's business model as an example of what was seen as a good business practice. Harvard Business School even wrote a case study on Enron. And the former dean of Stanford Business School joined Enron's board of directors. But it turned out that Enron's business practices were largely illegal. Financial statements were false. Key members of Enron's top management were imprisoned. The public accounting firm that had audited Enron's financial statements collapsed. There was embarrassment at Harvard Business School as well as in the business school community in general.

As well as listening, one needs to ask the relevant questions so that one can identify the appropriate next steps. The owner of a large shipping company, Kristian Jebsen, gave me a book on this topic by Warren Berger, *A More Beautiful Question* (2014). I would suggest there are at least four "levels" of listening: being attentive in the present; clarifying and interpreting meaning; providing empathy; acting generatively (Scharmer, 2009), or as Stephen Covey said, "most people do not listen with the intent to understand, they listen with the intent to reply" (Covey, 1986). Effective listening is all about being ready and willing to take action!

Key Learnings

A focus on *discipline* in decision-making, i.e., applying *both* proper analysis *and* one's own judgment are critical element of all business and academic decisions, including, of course, in the case of a first-class business school's curriculum. Meeting such a demand is certainly not easy, however. I recommend making use of a combination of specially tailored fact files/cases and experience-based simulations. Such cases might typically contain a mix of data for shedding light on a particular decision as well as excerpts of what a decision maker might see as possible options. Analysis and judgment are both called for! Specially tailored simulations might illustrate this duality too. Several of the relatively simple simulations suggested by Kahneman et al. (2019) might work here.

We have seen how the lack of a balanced approach can lead to suboptimal decisions, even business failure. Behavioral factors are perhaps more important than previously thought, as highlighted by Professor

11 Discipline and Integrity in Decision-Making

Kahnemann and his associates (Kahneman, 2011; Kahneman et al., 2019). Curriculum design would clearly benefit from the inclusion of more such studies and in-class discussions about their impact on better business decision-making.

Compulsory modules on ethically sound business practices and corporate social responsibility are taught in many business schools today. The antithesis of integrity and honesty is corruption. We have seen how the pursuit of personal enrichment plays out in newspaper headlines on an almost daily basis, both at the personal level as well as when it comes to entire governments. Personal greed is at the heart of much of this. There might even be entire systems of dishonest players acting together. It important to remember that one's reputation is a valuable asset, to be "protected"!

Part IV

Business Skills

This part consists of four chapters that discuss some of the key business skills that I feel are particularly critical when it comes to effective business strategy. This has to do with practicing networking, working at speed, enhancing innovations through proactivity and positivity, with a final chapter focusing on the importance of recognizing fundamental business cycles and managing accordingly, paying attention to the proper timing for engaging in a business, and knowing when to get out.

There seems to be no universal agreement when it comes to the factors that are particularly important for business success, however. Authors such as Peters and Waterman, Drucker, and Tollman and Morieux, for instance, have proposed other criteria. Peters and Waterman (1982), for example, propose eight characteristics of effective business strategy, including keeping administrative layers in the company to a minimum and sticking to core values. Drucker covered similar management practices in his seminal book *The Practice of Management* (1954). Tollman and Morieux (2014) propose that the key to success is to reduce business complexity. Smith, Lewis, and Tushman (2016) introduced the concept of "Both/And Leadership", or a way of seeing and managing the dynamic tension present in our complex world of work.

12

Networking: An Emerging and Ongoing Dictum

Networking typically refers to the making of connections between humans. But what do we mean by networking in the context of business and business school education? *Networks* or *network strategy* is typically related to subscription-based organizations, entailing subscriptions by customers to a service offering. Perhaps the most obvious example are newspapers that we subscribe to, where we typically renew our subscription on a regular basis, provided, of course, that we are satisfied with the value of the offering that is made available to us through this subscription. There are, of course, many other examples of subscription strategies. This type of strategy seems to be growing at a fast pace. Thus, exposure to network strategies should occupy a prominent part of modern business schools' curricula and not be tangentially treated as part of conventional marketing and/or strategy courses.

"Give More than You Take"

I have been centrally involved in at least four networking strategies, each of which will be briefly discussed below. But first, let us review some key aspects of networking strategies, both positive as well as negative.

© The Author(s), under exclusive license to Springer Nature Switzerland AG 2022
P. Lorange, *Learning and Teaching Business*,
https://doi.org/10.1007/978-3-031-14564-3_12

132   P. Lorange

- Stable Cash Flow: A relatively stable cash flow requires a majority of subscribers to renew their subscriptions once they have been signed up. We might call this relatively low *churn*. But there is generally another side to this, in that there is never complete certainty that a customer will renew! Thus, predicting a perfectly stable cash flow is almost impossible to do.
- Rapid Growth: Rapid growth can be achieved by taking advantage of the digital technologies available today. Digital technologies are particularly well-suited to network strategies. Marketing, for instance, can now be carried out relatively inexpensively and on a more scalable basis, say, by advertising on Facebook, Twitter, and/or LinkedIn. Potential customers can be reached all around the world fairly inexpensively. Maintaining links with prospects who have already been converted to customers is now also relatively easy. Developing and maintaining a stable digital platform or homepage is, of course, key to all of this.
- Asset Light: A network strategy might be seen as more "asset light," i.e., typically requiring less capital investment than physical manufacturing and distribution. However, considerable commitments of funds might still be needed when it comes to this type of strategy, particularly to develop and maintain the requisite software, platform, and/or an appropriate homepage.
- Quality and relevance: This is perhaps the most crucial mantra when it comes to network strategies. Most subscribers will evaluate the cost-benefits of their subscriptions on an ongoing basis. If many of them start to feel that the benefits do not measure up relative to the costs then the cancellation rate of subscribers will be likely to increase, i.e., "increased churn," less "stickiness," as we often say (McCraw & Tedlow, 1996). Clearly, therefore, the subscription rate should be kept at a reasonable level. Furthermore, it would normally *not* be prudent to increase the subscription price too frequently. What the "owner" of a network strategy can more directly influence on an ongoing basis, however, is the relevance and quality of what is being offered. Innovation is key! This constant requirement to "deliver" is, of course, normally a positive, keeping everybody sharp. The market will usually give a clear signal if anything is out of order, which can lead to growing

12 Networking: An Emerging and Ongoing Dictum   133

churn. Maintaining a high degree of attractiveness for members is thus essential!

* Added strength when the network grows: Since most expenses tend to be fixed, both when it comes to the maintenance costs of the service and software costs, the more subscribers there are in the network, the stronger it tends to become!

Even with all these factors in place, there can be challenges. Let us therefore briefly address a few of these that could potentially be negative:

* Predictability: We have already touched upon the potential lack of predictability when it comes to the cash flow that might be generated. This lack of predictability can make the implementation of an effective network strategy more difficult.
* Workload: Successful network strategies will require a lot of work, particularly during the initial stage when one's offering is being developed. It goes without saying that developing and maintaining high relevance/quality offerings requires a lot of effort. These offerings must also be given constant and ongoing attention. This calls for not only a high level of dedication, but also ample financial resources.
* Long-term view: As discussed, developing a viable network strategy typically requires a lot of time. Patience is needed. And the availability of sufficient funds to "stay the whole course" is key! Clearly, it can take a great deal of time to develop a reasonable subscriber base, i.e., to secure a reasonably positive cash flow. Also, as noted, since expenses tend to be more or less constant, whether one's income is high or low. Reaching break-even might not only take time, but also be quite expensive.

In spite of all of these potential difficulties, there seems to be no doubt that network-based strategies are here to stay. Why? The main reason has to do with the scalability issues offered by modern technology. Rapid growth with broad reach is now more feasible than ever before. Thus, relatively less expensive, more cost-effective strategies are becoming a reality. Network-based strategies typically open up opportunities to deliver better outputs and at a lower cost. Recent experiences during the

COVID-19 pandemic have not only underscored this but accelerated the general move in this direction. Network strategies must feature prominently in the way we lead today, in business as well as in academic institutions, and also to develop today's curriculum in more fundamental ways rather than as mere add-ons to conventional strategy or marketing approaches.

Examples of Network Strategies

Let us now discuss some examples of successful network strategies in which I have been involved.

Norwegian School of Business (BI)

I have already touched upon the network strategy that was developed at BI (Chap. 2), which involved establishing several regional campuses, with local leadership in quite autonomous ways, but also with curriculum design, course development, faculty training, library services, and so on offered centrally. While this strategy did not involve subscription payments by BI's students, good quality offerings combined with a reasonable tuition fee all made available near where students would live provided strong value relative to costs. BI was indeed highly successful.

Various educational experts perceived a lack of quality in this regional network, however. Government-driven certification processes, for instance, tended to be based on rather traditional considerations, i.e., focused on full-fledged traditional campuses with their own libraries and other facilities. This effectively led to a curtailment of BI's network. While the local campuses did undoubtedly add to the overall competitiveness of the region in which they were based, there were nevertheless strong forces calling for the discontinuation of regional campuses. The top management of Jotun, for instance, one of the world's largest paint and coatings manufacturers, located in Sandefjord, pointed out that the closure of the local BI campus there represented a substantial problem for the company. Attracting strong management talents to work at its headquarters, i.e., international families with children, would no longer be as easy.

Lorange Institute (LI)

Our students largely enrolled because of the perception that the Institute's educational offering provided good value for money. The crux of Lorange Institute's strategy was network based. However, here too there was probably too much of a gap between what was actually delivered at the Lorange Institute and what might be considered to be "solid acceptable practice." The difficulty of obtaining certification from leading accreditation boards also reflected this; in the end, Lorange Institute had only relatively limited success.

Lorange Network

Lorange Network (LN) had around 3200 subscribers by the end of 2021, at the point when it was taken over by IMD. While LN's strategy was successful, continuing as an independent entity would have required substantial additional efforts, particularly by me. I was not prepared to commit to this, especially given my relatively advanced age (78). Thus, the decision to integrate LN into IMD was made to ensure the long-term successful continued development of the network.

IMD

When I was the President of IMD, I seemingly had an ability to instill positive energy into this organization on a day-to-day basis. And I did not tire of practicing network thinking. A key to this was to try to give positive feedback, including congratulating and encouraging everyone who worked in the IMD organization, not just senior professors. For example, Mr. François Bassoux, a research associate at IMD, once received an award. Several weeks later, when I passed him on the walkway, I stopped to congratulate him. He later told the person he was with, Professor Jean-François Manzoni, who, incidentally, many years later became IMD's President, that he was impressed with my memory and attention to detail. My philosophy was to "try to always give more than I took," i.e., positive network thinking!

Marsoft

This Boston-based research firm focused on advising shipowners and banks that were active in shipping finance of likely shipping market scenarios. The company's aim was to put its clients in a better position to undertake successful shipping-related projects, both when it came to ordering new ships and purchasing second-hand ships or selling, as well as chartering ("in/out," "long/short"[1]). Clients subscribed to Marsoft's quarterly reports on dry bulk as well as tankers. I sold my shares in Marsoft in the early 2019. I was no longer involved, neither on the board nor as an investor.

Keystone

This Oslo-based firm provides support to academic institutions as well as to individual students globally. While the "customers" (academic organizations, students) do not subscribe to Keystone's services as such, many of them, particularly institutions, tend to be clients for long periods of time. The firm's generation of revenue is based on a network strategy philosophy. Maintaining a steady customer base, with relatively little churn, is key. I was on the board of Keystone for several years but stepped down in the spring of 2020.

Globalpraxis

A Barcelona-based management consulting firm specializing in route-to-market strategies for consumer-based companies. The bulk of this company's efforts has been built on analyzing how to become more efficient within the various specific markets in which a particular client operates. The firm has been able to develop a successful digital business model. This allows Globalpraxis to pursue a virtual network strategy. I exited in early 2021.

---

[1] Lorange (2020).

Broader Implications

Network-based thinking might also provide guidance for how entire societies might be organized. At the heart of this, there needs to be a good chemistry between the various societal groups, i.e., a desire to seek solutions that most see as beneficial, i.e., a "win-win" culture, rather than adopting more conflict-related approaches where some Individuals are clear winners and others are losers. One example of the latter is reflected in the way that growing nationalism seems to have become a polarizing factor (Mounk, 2022). Thus, the core of an effective network strategy, including a workable societal network-based order, should be a widely shared sense of partnership. An ideal would be relatively common thinking and values. If there is too great a degree of polarization, network strategies will typically not work all that well.

Networking thus seems to be about "openness," connecting people and projects. I have always attempted to do this, including meeting and greeting people, including strangers, wherever I am! I feel comfortable talking to anyone, giving out my business card, being widely accessible, and following up promptly. It is rewarding to meet so many people and to continue to connect with them. I nurture my network.

Networking implies linking up with other people, interacting with them physically and/or via thoughts or virtually. Writing a book or an article might be seen as a fitting example of an author attempting to network with his/her readers. I have written more than 20 books. While one rationale for doing this has been to better crystallize my thoughts, resulting in more clear-cut written outputs, I have always cherished this "distanced-based" network with my readers (Moore & Sonsino, 2020).

Key Learnings

So, there is no doubt that networking should be a key part of the way we do business, as well as how we lead the educational institutions of the future and develop their curriculums. Designing processes—in business as well as in educational institutions—entails a lot of networking. Effective learning is more likely to occur when there is networking clarity.

13

The Importance of Gaining and Maintaining Speed

Over the years, I have come to believe that it is vital to be speedy, particularly when conceiving and implementing strategies. In this chapter, I will illustrate ways of achieving this. Importantly, I believe that this issue will not only be relevant to the practices involved in leading a business or an academic institution, but also increasingly critical in the implementation of novel curriculum design. Indeed, what emerges might be quite similar to that proposed by Reid Hoffman and Chris Yeh in their famous book *Blitzscaling* (2018). Hoffman and Yeh see simplicity and clarity as central. There are also other key aspects, such as practicing "aggressive" entrepreneurship, which implies "going for it" when there is a window of opportunity and cutting down on bureaucracy. Being prepared to take some level of risk is also essential for maintaining speed, of course. To promptly address the inevitable and unexpected setbacks is critical. Getting bogged down in problems that accumulate by failing to confront them as they arise is, of course, unacceptable. Clearly, this type of evasion can be quite comfortable at times, but it can also "derail" the drive for more speed.

© The Author(s), under exclusive license to Springer Nature Switzerland AG 2022
P. Lorange, *Learning and Teaching Business*,
https://doi.org/10.1007/978-3-031-14564-3_13

Operational Clarity

Both when I headed up Norwegian School of Business (BI) as well as IMD, I felt that I had more or less full control over how each of these organizations was organized. In both cases, I always attempted to further simplify the organizational design to have a better chance of achieving clarity and, thus, gain speed. I did realize that such simplifications might lead to more work for me, not the least because of the higher degree of centralization that this implied. And I was pleased to find that this did not seem to demotivate key employees. At BI, for instance, the number of academic departments was reduced from more than 10 to 3. This allowed me to be more directional when dialoguing with each of the new department heads, both when it came to the overall direction of research and with regard to pedagogical issues. When I had been Chairperson of Wharton's Management Department some years earlier, with five different sub-clusters of faculty members (strategy, organizational behavior, labor relations, technology management, and entrepreneurship), I had come to realize that it was difficult at best and, in reality, almost impossible to come up with a meaningful overall strategy for the department.

At IMD, I intentionally eliminated all academic departments and instead encouraged individual faculty members to "self-organize" in small cross-functional groups, by specific academic programs (in teaching or research), or by client. Customers tend to value the overall impact of a given program, rather than those accruing from its various functional components. Continuity is often critical too. To enhance this, I eliminated the typical professorial hierarchical labels (assistant-, associate-, full professor). All were simply now professors. Organizational design supported operational clarity. This was also the case with key organizational processes, such as faculty reviews, the granting of incentives, criteria for recruitment, marketing of programs, and so on. This organizational model allowed for a deliberate and stronger focus on implementation.

"Citizenship" was seen as a key factor, above all when it came to granting bonuses. A faculty member would receive extra annual pay and bonuses based on documented research outputs and teaching excellence in addition to citizenship. The latter activity entailed participation in

13 The Importance of Gaining and Maintaining Speed 141

alumni activities, such as visiting local alumni clubs, being active on various school committees, being available to meet clients, as well as being involved in the interviewing of prospective new faculty candidates. Bonuses were to be seen as extra compensation, without the accompanying cost for the school in terms of contributions to faculty members' pension funds. Thus, bonus allocations were indeed fully variable costs for IMD. And the size of the overall annual bonus pool would depend on how well IMD ran in a given year. The distribution of the bonus pot was intentionally heavily skewed, with a relatively small number of faculty members receiving the bulk of the bonus incentives. A strong *eclectic* performance was the main objective. Being unilaterally a good researcher or teacher was typically not sufficient to trigger a bonus.

Strategic Clarity

According to the present head of IMD, Dr. Jean François Manzoni, I was usually quite clear when it came to the key strategic parameters that faculty and staff would have to follow, especially if they intended to continue to be employed by IMD. The aim was to come up with a clear and simple way of explaining and communicating IMD's strategy. This would help create a well-defined playing field for the various members of the organization. It was important for them to know the "dos" as well as the "don'ts" and to understand how the school would compete. Faculty members were not allowed to compete with IMD's course offerings of course. How was this enforced? The involvement of two or more IMD faculty members in private programs was typically not allowed. Faculty members all had to ask for permission regarding *any* kind of outside work, with their commitment to IMD's own work always coming first!

I would usually use just a few slides to communicate my points. To me, "less is more"! I also often repeated the message using the same slides, i.e., the power of repetition. And I never aspired to present more than, say, three key issues at any one time. All of this was to try to make communication clearer and to keep it relatively simple. This was based on my belief that individuals are normally not well equipped to absorb more than relatively simple messages. Cognitive limits had to be respected!

142 P. Lorange

Professor Vikas Tibrevalla from INSEAD is reported to have once said: "IMD is a bunch of perhaps mostly less than top-rated academicians but is being led by a great Dean." Flattering as this might be, I believe that this had a lot to do with the strategic clarity I tried to create. IMD's success was indeed based on a strategic focus, underscored by a drive for speed!

Perhaps the most effective way to maintain speed is to continuously keep one's focus on growth, by creating value through expanding rather than by cost-cutting. One cannot budget oneself for success! This is the way IMD operated under the auspices of the leadership trio of Dr. Jim Ellert, Senior Associate Dean, Philip Koehli, our CFO, and myself.

I always attempted not to be overly political, but rather to handle issues as they presented themselves, honestly and directly, to achieve what was best for IMD. It was key *not* to necessarily agree with the "last person going out of the office door." My Board Chairman for many years, Dr. Fritz Leutwiler (former head of Switzerland's National Bank) underscored this by stating in no uncertain terms: "We have hired you to lead the Institute, and *not* to go for personal popularity." In line with this, I never took on any private consulting assignments that might have overlapped with IMD's own business—my job was to give free advice to its trusted customers.

In retrospect, the fact that I had picked up a lot of effective academic leadership practices before coming to IMD—from my experiences at MIT, Wharton, as well as from BI—was probably significant. This allowed me to become a more effective leader at IMD, without relying too heavily on "trial and error." Most academic leaders, in contrast, have received only rudimentary training at best for their upcoming administrative tasks, thus often making them relatively ineffective.

Avoid "Micro-Management"

At IMD, I was particular about letting everyone who had specific responsibilities, particularly Dr. Jim Ellert, the Senior Associate Dean, and Mr. Philip Koehli, the CFO, "do their thing," without injecting myself too much into what they were doing. Equally, I tried to open up exciting

13 The Importance of Gaining and Maintaining Speed · 143

challenges for many by, for example, spearheading new initiatives, the innovative OWP program (Orchestrate Winning Performance) being one example. Professor Jan Kubes directed this program. The school's EMBA program, with Dr. Andy Boynton as its first program director, was developed in a similar way.

Another example comes from S. Ugelstad Shipping (SUS), where crews were left to largely run their ships themselves, managing their own procurements (lubrication oil, spare parts, food, etc.). But there was, of course, a shared computer program in place, allowing each ship to compare itself to others in the SUS fleet.

Immediate Follow-Up

At IMD, my many sales trips required immediate follow-ups to be effective. Clear and concise communication was key to speedy execution. The late Danish shipowner, Maersk McKinney Möller, taught me this above all else. He was famous for his prompt, minimalistic, almost telegraphic style in his follow-up memos and letters!

I always try to summarize meetings in follow-up e-mails. If not, it can often be incredibly hard to navigate oneself through all the details at a later date. A positive outcome of this is that it stimulates others and new angles almost always tend to emerge. By applying this sort of discipline, I seem to be able to maintain speed while also stimulating creativity through coping with complexity.

Saving time is important. This does not imply thoughtlessness, of course. Being inclusive, stimulating, encouraging, and giving helpful feedback all contribute to speed, "giving more than one takes"! But this should always be done in a friendly and not an impatient way. We should all work on the challenge of pacing ourselves. This is also essential for maintaining speed!

In general, it is important to attempt to simplify matters as far as possible, but without losing the essence of the meaning. Seemingly complex issues can often be boiled down to relatively few essential points. This is particularly important these days, when most of us face a shortage of time, generally preferring to get issues presented to us in digested forms.

144   P. Lorange

Leading, as well as good curriculum design, should be driven by the simplicity principle. I have always attempted to focus on the essential, reducing complexity to a minimum in my communication and writing, when presenting in meetings, as well as sharing in my teaching.

Key Learnings

We have seen that moving at speed is vital for taking advantage of opportunities. Speed is key! In some large organizations, perhaps most often in public organizations, this can be hard, particularly when a large number of people are involved in the decision-making process. There is typically a plethora of meetings where everyone will be eager to express their views or concerns. But are the decisions made actually any better for this? Sadly, reaching consensus when a large number of people are involved takes time! In the end, the upside of gaining speed can easily be lost due to extra bureaucracy, whether in the private or the public sector!

Individuals may have a tendency to "protect their own turf." The result, again, can be unnecessary delays, a waste of energy, and frustration. It goes without saying that many firms might be spared many of these sources of delay, assuming effective leadership from the top. Gaining speed entails more than clear operational focus, strategy, and structure, however. Speed implies "blitzscaling," indeed a whole mindset! (Hoffman & Yeh, 2018).

So, what are some of the key issues that need to be addressed in relation to speed in today's leadership and curriculum? We might remind ourselves of what Mr. Marvin Bower said in the title of his world-acclaimed book, *The Will to Manage* (Bower, 1966). Bower was the managing partner of the world-famous consulting firm McKinsey & Co. for almost two decades. Bower attributes speed to a manager's ability to cut through "red tape," to simplify, and also to be able to take some personal risks to "get things done." I am in line with Bower here, and so is the leadership philosophy and curriculum design that I am proposing. To recap, many organizations function in such a way that they fail to achieve sufficient speed. Why? My experience points toward these three considerations.

13 The Importance of Gaining and Maintaining Speed   145

* A culture that is too complex, too negative ("do not do this and that!")—what might be labelled a "political culture." Under these circumstances an executive can easily end up asking "what is in it for me?" or "should I take a career risk by sticking out my neck?" The result is often inaction and also endless debates before a compromise decision is reached, and this is often sub-optimal.
* An organizational structure that is too complex, often with matrixes, an abundance of committees to reach consensus, the need to secure agreement from many different departments or individuals, and so on. This typically results in delays! To simplify, organizations should flatten the "pyramids," removing layers, as well as creating more autonomy in "micro-organized," semiautonomous smaller entities.
* Lack of ownership, which is often found in family firms. A manager should perhaps have "skin in the game" to encourage speedy decision-making. Stock options can help, as having ownership stakes tend to be a good thing. But is not easy to allow managers to have a sufficient stake through stock options in the companies they lead, particularly when these are large, publicly traded firms.

I would recommend that businesses, as well as business schools, incorporate real-world examples, perhaps from well-run family businesses, into their curricula to illustrate how best to achieve speed. It would also be advisable to pay particular attention to the all-too-common dichotomy between strategy formulation and strategy implementation, which is often to blame when it comes to a lack of speed. Eliminating this dichotomy, an unnecessary complicating factor, should be at the core of strategic considerations and be squarely reflected in the strategy offered by all leading business schools also.

14

Proactivity, Positivity, and Innovation

We have already discussed the critical importance of innovations, as we saw it as a key success factor for implementing more effective network strategies—more "stickiness" to ameliorate churn. Innovations are indeed critical when it comes to creating effective strategies in general. A strong innovative drive seems to be key for firms to be able to maintain dominant positions. A strong focus on innovation is also key for "underdogs" to catch up. We saw an illustration of this in the evolution of the automotive industry, when General Motors (GM) took over Ford, none the least driven by innovations in marketing; how Toyota in turn bypassed the US-based producers by innovating a more cooperative operating style; how Tesla pulled off technological innovations in the electric car sector. Innovations in the future relating to self-driving cars will undoubtedly also lead to new "winners."

Being open-minded, positive, and proactive is critical for business success. Explicit willingness to try new approaches is essential. Good management practices call for this. Also, today's curriculum design should incorporate this approach: how do we see the *upsides* and *not* so much the

© The Author(s), under exclusive license to Springer Nature Switzerland AG 2022
P. Lorange, *Learning and Teaching Business*,
https://doi.org/10.1007/978-3-031-14564-3_14

148 P. Lorange

problems of defending the status quo! Positive, open-minded feedback is, of course, paramount here, encouraging learners to strive for a "can do" attitude by seeing things in new ways.

Examples of Open-Minded, Positive Thinking in Practice

We ran an Executive Network at Norwegian School of Business (BI) to which senior business executives, numbering around 20 senior leaders, were all personally invited. They met with a more or less equal number of faculty members. There was typically a short presentation by one faculty member, and then a short formal "response" from one of the business leaders. There were then informal discussions in small groups. The participants would be served wine or mineral water and "finger food." These meetings took place four times per year and typically lasted 1 ½–2 hours. Thinking "outside-of-the-box" led to valuable competitive insights in this "meeting place" setting.

Why do such meetings seem to work so well for bringing out positive thinking? One reason is that it seems to create loyalty among participants. Further, being able to offer know-how that is seen as relevant to everyone present is particularly critical. Sharing relevant, original research is key. It is also important for most of the (ideally all) participants to be *curious* to find out more about "best practice." Involving leading, cutting-edge firms adds a "credibility" effect. It is then easier to stimulate listening and a more open-minded style. The ultimate aim is to arrive at shared positions based on an exchange of sound judgments. Positivity drives this effective benchmarking. The members in a network must feel a degree of "safety" for this to happen, however. Hopefully, a good context might be established for pursuing innovations without fear.

When I ran a doctoral seminar on strategy at the Stockholm School of Economics (SSE), students seemed to have an excessive tendency to focus on weaknesses in their analysis of the articles assigned as readings. I ended up making a rule that participants would have to list at least three positives before coming up with any negatives. The students generally found

14 Proactivity, Positivity, and Innovation 149

this hard, in the sense that they had perhaps been trained to find weaknesses. In general, they seemed to be rather heavily geared toward this kind of critical approach. Readings should be assigned which bring across positive as well as negative views. Effective learning comes about more readily in this way. A curriculum should support a "can do" philosophy, rather than primarily focusing on constraints.

To illustrate this further, let me share a story that I was told by Professor Harvey Wagner at Yale. The famous Professor George Danzig, who came up with the seminal paper "solving" sets of multiple linear equations by applying so-called "linear programming," started as an undergraduate student of mathematics at UCLA. At the end of each session, his professor wrote down a problem on the board for the students to solve before the next class. For the last class of the semester, Dr. Danzig was a few minutes late. Thus, he did not hear the professor say, "this problem has never been solved and it never will be"! He simply copied the problem down and then went home to solve it! The message is clear: preconceived constraints should not be allowed to limit anyone's creativity.

Positive thinking is key at SUI too. All the decisions we make are unanimous between my son, my son-in-law, and myself. Should one sense that one or more members of the top team are uncomfortable with a particular decision, then we tend to drop the project. Decisions that some might find too controversial are simply not pursued. We recognize that we are going to have to work together for a long time—hence our positivism.

Innovation

Innovations are, of course, of critical importance when corporations are trying to ensure continued success. This has been researched extensively by many scholars. But the leading figure is perhaps Professor Charles Christensen of Harvard Business School, whose seminal contributions have been reported in numerous books and articles. His book *The Innovator's Dilemma* (1997) stands out here. He states that there are basically three types of innovations, listed here according to the degree of impact—from relatively small to extensive:

- Innovations to improve present practices and/or existing products.
- Innovations to leapfrog the competitiveness of an existing business activity, typically by businesses that are already established in this business segment.
- So-called disruptive innovations: Brand new ways of doing things, often with new players which are thereby able to outcompete players that have dominated a business segment through more conventional business models.

For all of these types of innovations, however, there seems to be a clear link to the customer, attempting to serve him/her in a better way, i.e., to enhance customer loyalty, "stickiness," and to reduce churn.

Coming up with better products or services is key. An example of this can be related back to the innovations we made at Lorange Institute, as discussed in Chap. 5. Here, we were able to develop an improved pedagogical approach, which probably resulted in better learning for the students. There were three core dimensions to the changes we introduced:

- The classrooms—smaller than normal auditoriums, with around 30 participants sitting around circular tables, the floors being flat.
- The pedagogical approach—a professor would raise key questions or issues, often distributed beforehand, and then lead a discussion around these, drawing on the students' own experiences and reflections as much as possible. The professor then attempted to summarize it all at the end of the discussion, including linking the insights that emerged to established bodies of knowledge. In this kind of arrangement, it is key to acknowledge the role of the professor as a conductor; listening to and stimulating the students. He/she learns too!
- Diversity—the students came from various backgrounds, nationalities, and experiences. Diversity was key. They spent several hours together when they met. Given that the course was supplementary to their full-time jobs, this was often on weekends. They were encouraged to stay in their jobs, to be active in their work life, while also studying. Modular curriculum design was essential, so that the various topics might be covered in concentrated ways. But the sequence of what is

14 Proactivity, Positivity, and Innovation

covered is probably less important. Curriculum design might have to be relaxed, to be less rigid.

The topic of cost containment was key. A prime feature here was to keep salary and pension costs under control, by employing professors for specific engagements in teaching or on research projects, rather than on a full-time basis. Administrative staff were also employed as consultants where possible, avoiding pension costs. Even the physical campus facilities could be kept smaller and simpler. What was key was proximity to transportation facilities (airport, rail), as well as accommodation.

Technology also plays a role, as we saw clearly with Lorange Network in Chap. 5. Scalability can lead to cost savings. We were able to offer webinars with cutting-edge educational content to our entire network of 3300 members. Classroom capacity and the human constraints of teaching staff no longer applied! Virtual pedagogy linked to distance learning also allows for the submission of papers on a regular basis, to check that students actually follow up on their learning tasks. This relates back to improved quality of learning as well as to cost-efficiency issues.

Let us now briefly discuss the growth of two other important innovations, both largely driven by technology, namely online shopping and working from home. Online shopping picked up substantially when COVID-19 pandemic restrictions were put in place. It turned out that as consumers got used to this, they also realized how convenient it was. The widespread practice of online shopping thus continues, even as the pandemic restrictions are lifted. "Players" such as Amazon, DHL, UPS, and the postal service are flourishing. It is all about technology-driven innovation! Finding ways to deliver a product or service at a lower cost is also a key driver of innovation. Being able to deliver a product or service which can perform better in terms of health, safety, and/or emissions is also important. We saw above, for instance, the impact of the severe global outbreak of the COVID-19 pandemic when it came to the emergence of innovations. And clearly, the emergence of new technology will play a role when it comes to innovations.

Working from home is another practice that seems to be set to continue. Initially, this was also driven by the pandemic. Interactions between those working from home via video conferencing tools have allowed for this way of working. We have seen considerable savings when it comes to the cost of office space as well as in air travel. The speed of business is picking up also and there was no longer much need for large office spaces.

In the end, it comes down to whether consumers at large are willing to adopt emerging innovations. Are the cost savings sufficiently high to persuade consumers to switch and possibly incur more uncertainty for themselves? Is the new cost difference sufficient to justify this? Timing is closely related to this. Many of us are creatures of habit and are reluctant to change unless there is some sort of dramatic external event that encourages us to do so. The pandemic was such an event.

The Scandinavian web-based online shopping firm, Co-Shopper, exemplifies this dilemma. While their concept of online shopping did well during the COVID-19 lockdowns and the aftermath, the concept was actually brought to market before the outbreak of the pandemic, and it did not succeed. Consumers did not switch to this approach at the time. The concept was perhaps launched a few years too early!

Key Learnings

It is all about innovation! We have seen how active "group think" can lead to positive outcomes. Thinking outside of the box seems to be a good thing. Positive feedback and praise are central elements here, leading to greater levels of self-confidence. As previously noted, a good rule of thumb is to attempt to "give more than one takes" (Polman & Winston, 2021). But surprisingly, there are relatively few people that can match up to this degree of positivism. There are implications here for effective administration practices, both in business as well as in academia. This also applies to design of an effective curriculum for the academic institutions of the future. An effective curriculum should be "light" when it comes to constraints. Innovations, to be effective, must be closely linked to such open-minded contexts. Hence, effective innovation, a positive outlook, and proactiveness go hand in hand.

15

Cycle Management: Entries and Exits

In most business applications, it is essential to take advantage of the underlying business cycles of the industry in which one operates. I experienced the benefits of this for the first time in shipping, first in my capacity as a board member of Olsen & Ugelstad Shipowners (O&U), Oslo, and subsequently as the owner of S. Ugelstad Rederi (SUR), Oslo. At the heart of good business cycle analysis is learning to buy when a particular cycle is on the low side, then ideally selling when the cycle is on the high side. So, it comes down to a matter of proper decision-making regarding "in/out," as well as "long/short," all driven by a basic "feel" for how the underlying market cycle might move.

The length of cycles in various industries can vary, of course. One example of an extraordinarily long cycle was recounted to me by the late Italian Count Cinzano, who stated that his Vermouth wine business seemed to enjoy a cycle of almost 100 years! Most business sectors are not blessed with such stability, however. There tend to be relatively shorter and distinct cycles that go up or down, depending on the market. And on top of this, there can be smaller, less pronounced cycles, which will almost always give rise to good cycle management opportunities, not only "in the large," but also "in the small"!

© The Author(s), under exclusive license to Springer Nature Switzerland AG 2022 **153**
P. Lorange, *Learning and Teaching Business*,
https://doi.org/10.1007/978-3-031-14564-3_15

154   P. Lorange

Decision-Making in Cycle Management

The importance of cycle management might best be illustrated by two early investments I made, both in Norwegian limited partnerships. One involved investment in a project with three handy-size bulk carriers, where I was forced to sell my share prematurely at the bottom of the cycle, incurring a loss. Back in 1981, I felt that I needed the cash to buy a house! But business cycles are not affected by this type of consideration. The other was when I invested in a relatively large bulk carrier, under a Mexican flag, which was bought when the market was perhaps too high. I ended up having to contribute additional funding when the ship's value subsequently fell, in line with a falling market. The call for additional capital was then triggered by covenants set by the debt financing banks. This was in 1986. Both examples illustrate how not being in sync with underlying cycles in certain markets will almost inevitably lead to losses. Cycle management is a central skill in a number of different contexts. Therefore, a focus on the correct analysis of cycles needs to be a key element of modern decision-making in business, as well as for today's curriculum.

Reaching satisfactory decisions on cycle management seems to depend on two fundamental considerations:

* Will a decision maker able to make rational decisions or is he/she locked into a cognitive trap fed by unrealistic expectations? Being rational under these circumstances is often easier said than done. Some managers may anticipate a continued upward movement when cycles go up, virtually forever! In contrast, downturns might also be seen as being likely to continue. A so-called "flock mentality" among decision makers may play a role in this type of thinking. I have to confess that, at times, I should also be included in this group of decision makers.

Let me, however, share with you one case where I did not fall into this trap, namely when I sold the ship assets in S. Ugelstad's Rederi. The market outlook seemed clear, being near the top of the cycle! My key shipbroker, Per Engeset from R.S. Platou, also indicated that we might be near the peak, as did my analysis of orders for new builds relative to ships in the water. However, when I decided to sell, my decision was met with general disbelief in my organization. Further, there was general skepticism in the industry. One prominent shipbuilder even indicated that I was not only wrong but that I was a total "woodskull"! This illustrates how difficult it might sometimes be to make such exit decisions. It may often be more comfortable to be part of the herd! However, this is not cycle management!

* Are there structural barriers in place? There can be powerful structural barriers to proper cycle management in many organizations. In many limited partnerships, for instance, there might be disagreements between board members, particularly when it comes to decisions about when to exit or whether to continue to go long on employment contracts.

In general, it seems that better decision-making, including an adaptation to cycle movements, can be achieved when there is *both* a relatively simple ownership situation *as well as* a relatively clear assignment of decision-making authority. Some shipowners, fund managers, or real estate investors function in this way, which is perhaps one of the main reasons for finding good cycle-driven practices in such firms. Further, these firms are often privately owned.

Examples of Cycle Management

Let us now look at cycle management issues in more detail in three industries, again reverting to shipping as our first example, then in real estate, and finally in the stock market. A general observation: listening to experts is key in each of these contexts. But good listening can at times be difficult. We might be more inclined to listen to inputs that confirm our own pre-formulated opinions! For this reason, it is useful to focus on objective indicators as far as possible. For instance, I analyzed the development of the ratio between new builds and ships "in the water" in the platform supply ship PSV ship segment. A combination of subjective assessment, good listening, and in-depth analysis represents a good guide to in/out, long/short decisions. Now onto three examples:

156   P. Lorange

Shipping

Two observations about the decisions taken during my time as a board member of the Oslo-based shipowners Olsen & Ugelstad come to mind. The first is that we often seemed to buy ships when they tended to be too expensive. The second observation has to do with a long-term charter that a large VLCC/OBO[1] carrier that O&U owned entered into. While the timing of this decision seemed to be relatively good, it turned out that the other party was unable (or unwilling) to honor the terms of the charter when the market subsequently went down. The financial strengths of a counterparty, as well as their reputation, should always be assessed when entering into "long" decisions. Are they likely to be strong enough to live with the consequences of a potentially deteriorating market, which is what they initially have agreed to do in the charter agreement? Do they have the cash?

To return to S. Ugelstad Rederi, which I wholly owned for a long time, the sale of an anchor-handling offshore supply ship is another example of inadequate cycle management by me. The ship was sold too early when the cycle was just about on its way up following a period of long-depressed prices, during which time the ship had been laid up. It was resold by the intermediary owner relatively quickly at a good profit for this owner. It was a significant loss of opportunity for me!

A second example relates to a platform supply vessel, the timing of the initial purchase having been good. However, the ship lacked the capacity to carry drilling mud. I turned down an offer to rebuild the ship with the necessary new tanks to be built when the freight market was down, which was also at a time when most shipyards' order books were relatively empty. The basic freight market also impacted prices in the shipbuilding market! When the market came back fairly soon afterward, the result for me was a considerable opportunity loss by not being able to provide a ship with the type of tank configurations that the market demanded! The cost of making such conversions at most shipyards had by then gone through the roof!

---

[1] "VLCC": Very Large Crude Carrier. "OBO": Oil, Bulk, Ore.

Real Estate

The purchase and subsequent sale of Lorange Institute is another example of good timing. I was able to purchase this lakeside property in Horgen, Lake Zurich in 2010. The real estate market was relatively low at that time. The purchase of an adjacent property, an abandoned water purification plant, was made subsequently. Both properties were then sold to CEIBS, a Shanghai-based business school, in 2017. It was clear that there had been an appreciation in property values. In addition, I had initially paid for the property with Norwegian kroner, transferred from Norway. The sale was transacted in euros, however, which have appreciated considerably. It became a good deal!

I have been involved in real estate investments in the USA (RCG), Switzerland (Turnqey), and Norway (Christiania Eiendomselskap and TopCamp). A common feature of all of these investments was a requirement to upgrade these relatively small rental properties, primarily through refurbishing. This made the timing of the "in" decision slightly less critical, in that the properties would typically achieve significantly higher market values through the upgrading. The Norwegian real estate investment consists of a plot of land for development (Christiania Eiendomselskap) as well as camping grounds (TopCamp), where the upgrading largely involves the installation of new sanitary facilities, improved shopping facilities, etc. Cycle management is essential when it comes to all entry, exit, or conversion decisions.

Stocks

My basic approach here has been similar to that of my investments in shipping and real estate, namely, to pick stocks that seem to be relatively cheap but have the prospect of an increase in value. Purchasing too early *or* too late may be suboptimal and thus expensive. Discipline is critical here too. Selling to "take profits" is often key. Some actors may find this difficult, perhaps due to extrapolative thinking. It can often make good sense to sell a portion of a given stock to recover one's original

158   P. Lorange

investment, enjoying a more or less free ticket from the holding that remains. Good timing is everything. Almost constant monitoring of a stock portfolio might be needed to take advantage of cycles.

The Timing of IPOs[2]

Valuation becomes central when investing in most venture projects. What will the "price tag" be for a particular project? Hitting the market is key, again an issue dictated by the appropriate business cycles. Reaching a realistic valuation, however, is never easy, particularly if there is not yet any revenue/sales data available for a particular project. How, then, do we price "a good idea"? A realistic understanding of the underlying cycles is central.

When going public, a promoter will typically want to push for a relatively high valuation, which will at times be unrealistic. Admittedly, coming up with a valuation that is in line with what the investor market finds reasonable can be difficult. Too high a stated evaluation price might mean that an IPO fails. The subsequent stock price may perhaps be lower than the IPO price was! Too low a pricing, on the other hand, might mean that the original owners might forgo some of their profit as part of the IPO process. It thus comes down to being able to judge the state of the market relatively accurately!

Key Learnings

We have seen that an understanding of market cycles can be vitally important for business success. Decision-making that takes into account the various stages of market cycles is essential for most businesses. It is therefore equally important to design a business school curriculum that covers the development of different scenarios for cycles as well as to expose students to accurate decision-making within the contexts of cycles.

---

[2] "IPO": Initial Public Offering.

15 Cycle Management: Entries and Exits

How might this be achieved? Let us go back to the "in-out/long-short" rule of thumb. This is a useful guide on how to manage in a cyclical world. Most businesses are exposed to such market swings. When markets are trending towards the bottom, it usually makes sense to buy. Conversely, when markets are at or near the top, it usually makes sense to sell, to "get out." We see this kind of cycle management in many types of business. Two types of ameliorating factors seem to stand out, causing potential problems—one being psychological, coping with flock mentality, the other having to do with finding relatively objective lead indicators to better understand cycle movements.

In terms of the psychological factors, having the discipline to act independently is a key to learning. One should avoid a so-called herd mentality. The use of good case studies might help learners to better understand this. As for lead indicators, it is particularly important to understand changing supply and demand trends in markets. In shipping, for instance, what do the new build order books look like? Are some ships/ship types likely to become obsolete and be withdrawn from the market? (Examples: single hull tankers, requirements regarding clean ballast tanks, and/or CO_2 emissions). Are certain macrotrends likely to affect the demand pattern, say, with fewer investments called for in new offshore oilfield development (making much of the existing fleet of offshore supply ships superfluous)? Is global trade likely to pick up? What about China's coal imports, given growing global ambitions to limit CO_2 emissions? A better understanding of such phenomena will be needed. The political reality is always key, and typically hard to predict.

Part V

Conclusions

Learning might indeed be a common label for much of what we have discussed in this book. Today's world requires individuals to learn more, faster, and better. Learning should also be taking place in the contexts of the business organization or the academic institutions in which we work. Modern curriculum design needs to reflect what we have learnt more recently! It may indeed be meaningful to think about learning organizations. There seems to be a race to learn faster, better and more in today's world. As stated in this book's introduction, my vision has been to come up with prescriptions for better decision-making both in business as well as in academia. Lifelong learning and higher executive education should not only become better, but also more cost effective to deliver. Several leading authors have pointed out that a vision should be relatively *simple* in order to be meaningful; there are, of course, several other elements to a realistic vision. My ventures, Lorange Institute and Lorange Network (Chap. 2), led to a further clarification of my vision concept, as did my business activities (Chap. 6) as well as my consulting and board experiences (Chap. 7). As already elaborated, various key events in my lifelong journey have led me to come up with new aspects of my vision. So, while

162 Conclusions

each of these insights can be traced back to what has been discussed in the various chapters of this book, they have perhaps not yet been spelled out as topical elements that might drive leading decision-making, or its parallel in academia, including how to inform a modern curriculum. The principles and skills I have highlighted should, of course, drive decision-making, perhaps even more than before, both in business as well as in academic institutions and also find their way into the modern curriculum.

16

Learning in the Future: Individuals, Business, and Academic Institutions

Part One of the book attempts to shed light on the people and events that have contributed to my thinking about effective decision-making and curriculum design via a series of autobiographical highlights. While, at first glance, some of the personal experiences may not seem directly relevant, I do not necessarily agree with such a conclusion. But rather than repeating various aspects of this part of the book, let me instead offer an alternative interpretation of some of the key steps in the development of my thinking. For this, identifying trends that will shape the future are important, highlighted in the discussion below. One might end up more or less where one wanted, even though our world is clearly not organized in such a predictable way. There is, of course, no certainty that one will reach one's desired targets. Nevertheless, it seems key to always try to position oneself in such a way to have a better chance of ultimately reaching one's goal. Let us look at several events from my own "journey" which potentially might confirm this:

* Being admitted to Norwegian School of Economics and Business Administration (NHH). When I applied for admission in 1962, it was next to impossible to get in. But studying hard both at high school and at junior college seemed to make a difference.

© The Author(s), under exclusive license to Springer Nature Switzerland AG 2022
P. Lorange, *Learning and Teaching Business*,
https://doi.org/10.1007/978-3-031-14564-3_16

- Being admitted to the doctoral program at Harvard Business School. I was rejected in 1967 the first time I applied, but was admitted to the doctoral program in operations analysis at Yale instead. As I gradually came to feel that the program at Yale focused too much on advanced mathematics for my taste, I settled for a master's degree at Yale. This degree seemed to have been an effective door-opener to Harvard's doctoral program and I was admitted in 1968.
- Academia. Hard work at IMEDE, from 1971 to 1973, contributed to me entering a professional career at the Sloan School of Management, MIT. Later on, this probably paved the way for me to become a faculty member at Wharton. Then later, my cumulative experience at Sloan and Wharton made it relatively easier for me to be elected as President of Norwegian School of Business (BI) in Oslo. The fact that I already had had a relatively successful administrative academic career at BI probably made me, in turn, a more attractive candidate to become president at IMD.
- The sale of Lorange Institute. This project was relatively successful. Having been a board member of EFMD, which owned part of CEIBS business school in Shanghai, it was a natural step for me to sell Lorange Institute to CEIBS in 2016.
- I then launched Lorange Network (LN) in 2018, a digitalized service intended to offer learning support primarily to family firms and independent investors. It gradually became clear to me, however, that continuing to run Lorange Network would be unrealistic in the long run. My former employer, IMD, offered to take over Lorange Network at the end of 2021.
- My own extensive research publications have shed light on effective business strategies and leadership practices, both in business as well as in academia. It is important to reiterate the importance of research here. Without this, I would undoubtedly have been ill-equipped to come up with an overall synthesis. There are still many issues that remain unanswered. More research is needed.

There seems to be an accumulation of insights, new learning, that has driven the evolution of my vision behind each step on this journey. This accumulation, an increasingly more advanced vision through learning

16 Learning in the Future: Individuals, Business, and Academic... 165

from experience, seems to have put me in a position to be more ready for each career step. This may not be merely coincidental!

What I draw from this is that hard work is equally essential for things to fall into place. Shortcuts and compromise do not work when striving for quality! It is undoubtedly also the case that a great deal of learning took place along the way, increasing the likelihood of my being in a position to seek new challenges. For instance, the administrative experience I gained at Wharton made me better qualified to take on the assignment as President of BI. And this experience, in turn, probably qualified me to take on the assignment as President of IMD. Thus, having gained insights into the management of business schools, I was probably in a better position to embark on experiments, both at IMD, and subsequently with entirely new business models in order to develop more efficient learning at Lorange Institute and then at Lorange Network.

Let us elaborate further on some of the lessons learned from Part Two. A key lesson is to make use of emerging technology to its fullest. This can lead to significant cost savings by allowing businesses to be run more effectively. This has indeed been my experience, both with S. Uglestad's Rederi (SUR) and S. Ugelstad Invest (SUI). In academia, technology will allow us to take advantage of new scale opportunities since conventional classrooms and lecturers/professors are no longer limiting factors. Virtual/distance learning opens up a new reality when it comes to lowering costs. And the quality of the learning process is probably higher too, allowing students to combine learning with their jobs, thus being in a position to draw on their real-life experiences. We saw that with Lorange Network as well as Lorange Institute. More diversity, geographically, in particular, might also be beneficial. Particular elements of what is being covered might easily be revisited, but with a wider geographic context in mind. Virtual exams, papers, and exercises can effectively guard against free riding, which elsewise might be a potential problem.

The power of innovation is illustrated throughout this book. When it came to how S. Ugelstad's Rederi was run, for instance, each ship's crew was given a wider responsibility than is generally expected—more self-governance. The positive behavioral factor, with extra motivation, that resulted from this innovative practice was impressive.

166   P. Lorange

The benefits of the power of portfolio diversification are clear, as perhaps illustrated so well when it comes to S. Ugelstad Invest. Diversification, within its limits of course, did indeed enhance overall performance and a better management of exposure to SUI's risk.

Also, both when it came to my work on boards, as well as in my consulting, I have attempted to always support existing management, to "help" rather than to disrupt. This might be a quite distinct, even somewhat unusual approach, but is certainly gratifying.

It is important to preserve one's "energy," so as not to spread oneself too thinly and to avoid being caught up in too many conflicts and legal disputes. Such disputes and legal wranglings easily end up as a distraction. We saw the dysfunctional effects of legal disputes at Olsen & Ugelstad Shipowners, for instance. This ship owning company, co-founded by my grandfather, Rudolf Ugelstad, was for a long time one of the largest ship owning groups in Norway, as well as being a pioneer when it came to opening up new shipping routes, such as on the Great Lakes–Europe cargo route. But the company eventually faltered, not least due to a severe dispute between one of the members of the next generation with the other five members of that generation. The dispute lasted for more than a decade. This dispute, involving several court cases, took a lot of the top management's attention, and significantly lessened its focus on the business. These are merely my opinions, of course. But a key lesson seems to be that legal disputes should be avoided, if at all possible, so that top management's attention might be channeled in a direction that fully supports the business. Being successful in business is hard enough as it is! Being bogged down in court cases that distract top management simply makes it even more difficult! It would be beneficial to cover this topic more specifically in business school's curriculum. Students should be made aware of the value of steering clear of these types of conflicts. It is generally more important to focus instead on "positive energy," as I also discussed in Part Four.

Business Schools of the Future: Effective Curricula

There are at least three different issues that I believe should dominate the design of effective curricula:

Support Good Business Practices This is largely a matter of discussing key decision-making routines and emphasizing the quality of these. Being realistic and focusing on diversity should be emphasized throughout the course. A program of studies should also be inspirational, productive, and positive. Discipline, honesty, and integrity should be emphasized, as we saw in Part Three. And good leadership practices in business generally also apply to the management of academic institutions.

Instill a Strong Sense of Dynamism Perhaps the most critical issues to explore are new ways to gain speed, to reduce bureaucracy, and to come up with better timing for one's strategies through a clearer understanding of cycle management. Dynamics are driven by the key forces of the business cycles, i.e., not by our own preferred choices. Students should get a good sense of how to outperform the competition in this way. A thorough exposure to risk and uncertainty should also be prominently featured. The networking context is critical here. Network-based organizations need to be dynamic, and they are becoming more and more dominant in management practice. As a result, the curriculum should include comprehensive coverage of networking. It is, perhaps, a common misconception that this type of focus on networking entails a lack of stringency, or even sloppiness! This is not so, as we saw in Part Four above all.

Participate and Listen Most of us will have real-life experiences that should be drawn on in learning situations. Inviting students to share their experiences will typically lead to an increased sense of participation, "giving and taking." Encouraging students to bring to the table their experiences and what they feel is critical is key. This will also strengthen their self-confidence, another important part of learning.

There are several particularly relevant implications from the above when it comes to how learning interactions might be structured. Above

168   **P. Lorange**

all, there are three overriding considerations to be kept in mind—issues surrounding the delivery of content and how the learning process itself might be structured.

The Professor His/her main task should be to raise issues for discussion and lead debates with students in contrast to the more traditional role of "one-way" lecturing, delivered from the "pulpit." Such discussions could be run virtually, with each student participating remotely, or they could take place in specially designed classrooms. Typically, these would be longer sessions. Here are some of the key tasks to keep in mind:

* Propose an agenda for the topics to be discussed. This should be linked to assigned reading materials that have been distributed beforehand. Students should also be invited to provide inputs to the agenda and to lead discussions, in an inclusive way. Experience suggests that some students will contribute more than others. An effective professor should encourage all students, and, of course, discourage those who would otherwise dominate the session.
* Articulate conclusions regarding the intended key learning points. Ideally, professors would no longer deliver what we might consider traditional lectures, with information travelling in one direction. Rather, he/she might be compared to some sort of conductor, like in an orchestra. Two-way learning can then more easily take place, but with the interaction clearly structured. Significantly, in this approach a professor often becomes a learner too! (Argyris, 1999). Finally, effective professors summarize the key learning points at the end of the session. Follow-up notes or summaries further highlight the learning.

Classroom Setting Students should be able to see and hear each other with ease. Facial expressions and tone of voice are important! Most traditional classrooms thus normally need to be redesigned, eschewing horseshoe-shaped amphitheater layouts for "flat rooms." These might have round tables, with six to eight students being seated around each. Students would then also be able to cluster in groups. There might, say, be five tables in a given room, with 30–40 students participating in total. In virtual learning settings there will, of course, be no classroom. Students should be able to observe each other on their screens. Here too, the students might be arranged into smaller groups.

Modularity It is going to be increasingly important for students to be able to do their studies while also keeping their full-time jobs. Shorter, relatively more intense learning modules seem to have become more of the norm. Utilizing weekends as well as vacation periods is becoming more common. The use of virtual learning to complement learners' physical presence on campus will further accelerate this trend in learning, i.e., a mix of campus-based and remote learning. There should be a lot of flexibility when it comes to the sequencing of the learning modules. For instance, while a student might traditionally have had to study basic accounting before advancing to taking a module in finance, such rigid sequencing might no longer be necessary. There is an abundance of opportunities for self-study, open to individual students who might have particular needs, thereby allowing for much greater flexibility in sequencing. A greater degree of user-friendliness might be the result!

Modern Organizations and Educational Institutions: Principles and Skills

There are perhaps five heuristics that are particularly critical for modern organizations to pay attention to, all with roots in research, and each being significant for the design of effective business institutions as well as for those undergoing higher learning.

* "When in doubt, do the right thing." While this aphorism was perhaps first coined by General Norman Schwarzkopf, the successful commander of the United States-led force that occupied Iraq in 1991, there is no doubt that outputs from research can help many of us to make the "right choices"! (Schwarzkopf, 1992; Polman & Winston, 2021).
* "We, we, we, *not* me, me, me." The validity of this has been confirmed in many studies. It has also been emphasized by many others, including Charles Koch and Paul Polman of Unilever fame (Koch & Hooks, 2020; Polman & Winston, 2021). The fundamental reality behind the dictum is perhaps a call for more research, so as to make this happen.

- "Strategy means choice" (Lorange, 2021). There are of course legions of strategic choices available to organizations at any point in time. Research might help us to understand which particular strategy to choose. Again, research can probably guide us even further here. The focus would be on the process of choice! No strategies can exist without an emphasis on choices.
- "Timing is all." I have emphasized many times that most businesses evolve through cycles. How to decide "when to get in/when to go long" and "when to exit/when to go short" is key. More research on business cycles might be needed, including cases based on "typical" cycle-driven industries such as banking, real estate, and shipping which might help us to gain additional insights.
- "Good can always be done better." This dictum is self-evident, but perhaps hard to practice without the support of further research.

Coming up with more effective ways to learn is, of course, the ultimate goal for both research as well as practical experimentation into higher education. The overarching aim of this book is to contribute to this. I have attempted to link experiences from my own life and career to this. Similarly, research activities in which I have been active may shed light on ways of coming up with more effective learning. Curriculum design represents the culmination of all of this.

Final Words

This book attempts to bring together some of my experiences and insights gained about better business management and also the leadership of academic institutions together with their impacts on curriculum design. I have attempted to shed light on what might constitute effective practices in business as well as in academic institutions of the future. Three complementary "lenses" have been particularly important for me, in this respect. First, I have drawn on autobiographical experiences. Second, I have given the reader an overview of my own research in this field. Third, I have reviewed good management practices. As previously noted, my career has been fundamentally dualistic in nature—focusing on both

16 Learning in the Future: Individuals, Business, and Academic... 171

academia and business. This may perhaps have qualified me to discuss such challenges of proper strategic leadership in a more effective way. The key has been to strive toward seeing these issues from complementary angles, rather than to concentrate on just one particular aspect. My business activities are undoubtedly relevant to the discussion but my deep involvement in business and academia is also key! There is a definite advantage to this kind of eclecticism here. The two strains, academia and business, have positive impacts on each other. This is critical when it comes to creating better and more cost-effective ways of leading, in business and in academia. This "multiple lens" viewpoint has helped me to gain new insights regarding what constitutes effective practices.

The main purpose of this book has been to stimulate new ideas about business leadership as well as within academic institutions. In the first part of the book, I have shared with readers some of the more significant learning points drawn from my career journey. I have also drawn some conclusions based on my own research efforts. Further, I have looked at some of the practices that I in particular have come to consider as contributing to good management. Throughout the book, I have tried to combine my personal and professional experiences. It is thought provoking how intertwined these two "lives" are! I hope that the reader is left with greater clarity, as well as a strong sense of optimism, after having read this book. The revolution in leadership, in business, as well as in higher education is continuing at an accelerated speed!

Books Authored

Strategic Planning

Behavioral Factors in Capital Budgeting, (1973), Universitetsforlaget.
Strategic Planning Systems (with Richard F. Vancil), (1977), Prentice-Hall.
Corporate Planning: an executive viewpoint, (1978), Prentice-Hall.
Implementation of Strategic Planning, (1982), Prentice-Hall.
Strategic Control, (with Michael S. Scott Morton and Sumantra Ghoshal), (1986), West Publishing.
The Challenge of Cooperative Ventures, (with Johan Roos), (1987), Stockholm School of Economics.
Cooperative Strategies, (1988), Emerald.
Cooperative Strategies in International Business, (ed. with Farok J Contractor), (1988), Lexington Books.
Managing the Strategy Process: A Framework for a Multibusiness Firm, (with B. Chakravarthy), (1991), Prentice Hall.
Strategic Alliances: Formation, Implementation and Evolution, (1992), Blackwell.
Implementing Strategic Processes: Change, Learning and Cooperation, (ed. With B. Chakravarthy, J. Roos and A. Van de Ven), (1993), Basil Blackwell.

© The Author(s), under exclusive license to Springer Nature Switzerland AG 2022
P. Lorange, *Learning and Teaching Business*,
https://doi.org/10.1007/978-3-031-14564-3

174   **Books Authored**

Strategic Planning and Control, (1993), Basil Blackwell
Cooperative Strategies and Alliances, (ed. By Farok J. Contractor), (2002), Pergamon.
Strategy Processes/Shaping the Contours of the Field, (ed. B. Chakravarthy, G. Mueller-Stewens, C. Lechner), (2002), Blackwell Publishing.
Thought Leadership Meets Business, (2005), Cambridge University Press.
Profit or Growth: Why you don't need to choose, (with B. Chakravarthy), (2007), Wharton Press.
Leading in Turbulent Times, (2010), Emerald.
From Great to Gone, (with J. Rembiszewski), (2014), Gower/Routledge

Educational

New Vision for Management Education, (2002), Emerald.
The Business School in the 21st Century, (with H. Thomas & J. Sheth), (2013), Cambridge University Press.
The Business School of the Future, (2019), Cambridge University Press.
Executive Education after the Pandemic, (with S. Iniguez), (2021), Palgrave.

Shipping

Shipping Company Strategies, (2005), Emerald.
Shipping Strategy: Innovating for Success, (2009), Cambridge University Press.
Innovations in Shipping, (2020), Cambridge University Press.

Family Business

Adaption and Flexibility in the Family Firm: A brief history of S. Ugelstad Invest, (2019), Smøyg Forlag.
Reinventing the Family Firm, (2021), IMD.

References

Aaker, D. A. (2008). *Spanning silos: The new CMO imperative*. Harvard Business Review Press.

Affenposten. (2021, September 10). *Samfunustoppene Svever*.

Allen, D. (2011). *The 6 horizons of focus* [online]. https://gettingthingsdone.com/2011/01/the-6-horizons-of-focus/

Anker, P. (2020). *The power of the periphery*. Cambridge University Press.

Argyris, C. (1999). *On organizational learning*. Blackwell Business.

Austen, J. (1999). *Seldom, very seldom*. Modern Library.

Berger, W. (2014). *A more beautiful question*. Bloomsbury.

Bjørnsson, B. (1992). *Fremmed, Verdens Gang*, reprinted. In Ø. Anker (Ed.), *De Gode Gjerninger*. Gyldendal.

Blas, J., & Farchy, J. (2021). *The world for Sale*. Penguin Random House.

Bower, M. (1966). *The will to manage*. McGraw-Hill.

Brabeck-Letmathe, P., (2020), Ascensions, Favre.

Brennan, N. M. (2016). *Shades of grey: Directors' dilemmas*. Institute of Chartered Accountants of Scotland.

Brown, D. J. (2013). *The boys in the boat*. Penguin.

Covey, S. R. (1986). *The 7 habits of highly effective people*. Free Press.

Chakravarthy, B., & Lorange, P. (2007). *Profit or growth, why you dont have to choose*. FT Press.

Christensen, C. M. (2013). *The innovator's dilemma*. Harvard Business Press.

© The Author(s), under exclusive license to Springer Nature Switzerland AG 2022
P. Lorange, *Learning and Teaching Business*,
https://doi.org/10.1007/978-3-031-14564-3

176 References

Dewar, C., Keller, S., & Malhotra, V. (2022). *CEO excellence: The six mindsets that distinguish the best leaders from the rest*. Schribner.

Drucker, P. F. (1954). *The practice of management*. Harper Business.

Elliot, T. S. (1931). *Transit of venus*. English Lion.

Freedman, L. (2013). *Strategy: A history*. Oxford University Press.

Hamel, G., & Prahalad, C. K. (2005). *Strategic intent*. Harvard Business Review.

Hoffman, R., & Yeh, C., (2018), Blitzscaling.

Jaffe, D. T. (2020). *Borrowed from your grandchildren*. Wiley.

Kahneman, D. (2011). *Thinking*. Fast and Slow.

Kahneman, D., Slovic, P., & Tversky, A. (2019). *Judgement under uncertainty: Heuristics and biases*. Cambridge University Press.

Konovalov, O. (2021). *The vision code: How to create and execute a compelling vision for your business*. Wiley.

Koch, C., & Hooks, B. (2020). *Believe in people*. St. Martin's Press.

Lahlum, H. O. (2019). *Reiulf Steen*. Cappelen Damm.

Lehrer, J. (2009). *Proust was a neuroscientist*. Houghton Mifflin Harcourt.

Lehrer, J. (2010). *How we decide*. Houghton Mifflin Harcourt.

Lindholm, M. R., & Møller, K. (1997). *Slip danskerne løs. Danmark efter informationssamfundet*. Aschehoug.

Lorange, P. (2008). *Thought leadership meets business*. Cambridge University Press.

Lorange, P. (2019a). *A brief history of S. Ugelstad invest (SUI)*. Smøyg.

Lorange, P. (2019b). *The business school of the future*. Cambridge University Press.

Lorange, P. (2020). *Innovations in shipping*. Cambridge University Press.

Lorange, P. (2021). *How to manage family-owned portfolio firms*. IMD.

Lorange, P. (2022a). *What makes a business a masterpiece?* Publisher unconfirmed.

Lorange, P. (2022b). *Art and business strategy: Peter Lorange's art collection*. Publisher unconfirmed.

Lorange, P., & Norman, V. D. (1973). *Shipping management*. Institute for Shipping Research, NHH.

Lorange, P., & Rembiszewski, J. (2016). *From great to gone*. Taylor & Francis.

McCarthy, A. (1971). *Private faces, public places*. Curtis Books.

McCraw, T. K., & Tedlow, R. S. (1996). *Henry ford, Alfred Sloan and the three phases of marketing* (pp. 1-796–1-169). Harvard Business Press.

Merckelback, S. (2020). *Source*. Aquilae Editions.

Mintzberg, H. (1994). *The rise and fall of strategic planning: Reconceiving roles for planning, plans and planners*. Free Press.

Moore, J., & Sonsino, S. (2020). *You should write a book*. MSL Publishing.

Moore, M. (1967). *The poems of Marianne Moore*. Penguin Publishing.

References   177

Mounk, Y. (2022). *The great experiment: How to make diverse democracies work*. Penguin.

Pabrai, M. (2007). *The Dhandho investor: The low-risk value method to high returns*. Wiley.

Peters, T., & Waterman, R. H. (1982). *In search of excellence*. Collins.

Polman, P., & Winston, A. (2021). *Net positive*. Harvard Business Press.

Popper, K. (1935). *The logic of scientific discovery*. Julius Springer.

Rorty, R. (1989). *Contingency, irony and solidarity*. Cambridge University Press.

Rumelt, R. (2011). *Good strategy, bad strategy*. Random House.

Scharmer, O., (2009), Theory U–leading from the future as it emerges, Berrett-Koehler.

Simon, H. (1992). *Economics, bounded rationality and the cognitive revolution*. E. Elgar Publishing Company.

Schwarzkopf, H. N. (1992). *It doesn't take a hero*. Bantam.

Smith, W. K., Lewis, M. W., & Tushman, M. L. (2016). *"Both/and" leadership*. Harvard Business Review.

Snabe, J. H., & Trolle, M. (2019). *Dreams and details*. Sprintype.

Tenold, S. (2018). *Norwegian shipping in the 20th century*. Springer.

Tollman, P., & Morieux, Y. (2014). *Six simple rules: How to manage complexity without getting complicated*. Harvard Business Review Press.

Towl, A. (1969). *To study administration by cases*. Harvard Business Press.

Vogel, P., (2020), Family philanthropy navigator, IMD.

Weber, M. (1905). *The protestant ethic and Spirit of capitalism*. Translated by Baehr, P., & Wells, G. C. (2002). Penguin Books.

Wernerfelt, B. (1984). A resource-based view of the firm. *Strategic Management Journal, 5*, 171–180.

Young, S. (2012). *Train your brain to focus*. Harvard Business Review. [online]. https://hbr.org/2012/01/train-your-brain-to-focus

Printed in the United States
by Baker & Taylor Publisher Services